HOPE IN TH...
a...
THATCHER'...

Trevor Griffiths's first full-length... produced by the RSC; *The Party* was premiered by the National Theatre, and his 1975 play *Comedians* moved from Nottingham to the National Theatre at the Old Vic and later to Broadway. More recently, his work for the theatre has included *Piano* for the National Theatre; *The Gulf Between Us*, a controversial appraisal of the Middle East conflict from an Arab perspective; and *Thatcher's Children*, a damning indictment of the Eighties produced by Bristol Old Vic.

Griffiths has also written extensively for television and was given the BAFTA Writer's Award in 1982. His 1976 political drama serial *Bill Brand* was followed by a wide-ranging series of pieces including the highly-praised *Country* and *Oi for England*, his anatomy of skinhead culture, as well as his adaptation of Lawrence's *Sons and Lovers* and his epic series about the race for the South Pole, *The Last Place on Earth*. *Hope in the Year Two*, a film for BBC Television about the French Revolution, was transmitted in May 1994. His work for the cinema includes *Reds* with Warren Beatty, for which he received an Oscar nomination in 1981, and *Fatherland*, which was directed by Ken Loach and premièred at Cannes in 1986.

HOPE IN
THE YEAR TWO
and
THATCHER'S
CHILDREN

Trevor Griffiths

faber and faber
LONDON · BOSTON

First published in 1994
by Faber and Faber Limited
3 Queen Square
London WC1N 3AU

Set in Linotype Plantin by Parker Typesetting Service, Leicester
Printed in England by Clays Ltd, St Ives plc

Introduction and text © Commonty Productions Ltd, 1994

Trevor Griffiths is hereby identified as author of this work
in accordance with Section 77 of the Copyright, Designs and Patents Act

All rights whatsoever in this play are strictly reserved and
applications for permission to perform it, etc., must be made
in advance, before rehearsals begin, to The Peters, Fraser and
Dunlop Group Ltd, 503/4 The Chambers, Chelsea Harbour, Lots Road,
London, SW10 0XF

A CIP record for this book
is available from the British Library

ISNB 0–571–17308–X

2 4 6 8 10 9 7 5 3 1

CONTENTS

Introductory Note and Dedication
page vii

HOPE IN THE YEAR TWO
page I

THATCHER'S CHILDREN
page 41

INTRODUCTORY NOTE AND DEDICATION

For all their differences – of tone, terrain and temper – these are plays cut from the same cloth. Both were conceived, set up, researched and written side by side over the year that followed the last general election. Both set fearsome problems for actors and directors, not least in discovering how to present a theatre piece for the screen (*Hope in the Year Two*) or a screenplay for the stage (*Thatcher's Children*). Each constitutes a raid on the past, an address to the present and a rejection of the future currently on offer. I'm delighted to see them published under one cover.

Thatcher's Children is dedicated to the company of young actors under Andy Hay at the Bristol Old Vic who workshopped their lives into my structures with such generous grace and unswerving verve and never once said no.

I dedicate *Hope in the Year Two* to Edward Thompson, whose work, life and beliefs have set a benchmark for us all. He's greatly missed.

Trevor Griffiths
January 1994

HOPE IN THE YEAR TWO

Hope in the Year Two was first broadcast on 11 May 1994 on BBC2.

PRISONER: Jack Shepherd
HENRY: Tom Bowles
LOUISE: Sophie Linfield

Director Elijah Moshinsky
Producer Ann Scott
Executive Producer Bill Bryden
Designer Haydn Griffin
Photography Ivan Strasburg
Music Carl Davis
Editor Ken Pearce

A theatre curtain. A city clock strikes two. The curtain opens.
Reveals a safety curtain. The painted blade of a guillotine all but
covers it. Bleed in man's voice, as if from sleep, lifting and falling in
the battle for coherence.

VOICE: **Who** . . .

> Don't read me lectures on how this tribunal shall proceed,
> Fouquier-Tinville, I created this bloody Tribunal, dreamed
> it up . . .
> **Shall** . . .
> Vadier sends Danton a message: tell that fat turbot, we'll
> gut him soon enough . . .
> **Be** . . .
> Danton answers: Tell Vadier, one step in my direction, I'll
> cleave his head open, suck his brains out and shit in his
> empty skull . . .
> **Happy** . . . o
> (*The curtain and the blade have creaked slowly up.*
> *Night. A grande salle of the requisitioned Luxembourg royal*
> *palace, vast, decrepit.*
> *A large metal-barred cage fills its centre. In it, prone on a*
> *bier-like divan, a solitary prisoner, asleep as if embalmed.*)

VOICE: (*Tape relay, then actor sharing, from sleep*) . . . Vadier
meant it. Danton didn't . . .

> **Who shall be happy** . . . ?
> No matter.
> **Who shall be happy** . . . ?
> (*Prison noises, sudden, resonant: locks, steps, a voice, another.*
> *The* PRISONER *is up, alert; listens: nothing untoward.*
> *Approaches the bars. Stares out into the dark.*)

PRISONER: . . . Still there? Aye, I see ye. Little white faces in
the dark. The future we are hatching here. Fell asleep.
Tired. Little white faces in the dark. Waiting to be born.
Where was I? Had I reached Paris yet? It doesn't matter.

I

Touch any part you touch the whole . . .

(*A door slams. The* PRISONER *lifts a lamp to watch a young guard shuffle awkwardly in, musket on shoulder, Phrygian bonnet rouge, ill-fitting boots, a tray of food in his hands. He spends some time finding nowhere to put it, finally lays it down on the floor, begins to head off.*)

PRISONER: (*Out into the dark; indicating guard*) As you see, we have begun upon experiments . . . Henry is but the first fruiting. The new citizen, the new man . . .

(HENRY *has stopped, slowly turns to watch.*)

HENRY: (*Finally*) What?

PRISONER: Did I speak?

HENRY: Don't start that. (*He watches on a moment, clumps off into the dark far reaches of the Salle to gather something.*)

PRISONER: I've got him thinking I'm the Madman. Apparently there are two of us. It seems the Committee, fearing a rescue plot, have summoned up a second Danton from a neighbouring asylum and had him caged, identically alone, in the Conciergerie, to confound the plotters. I came in a sealed coach and hooded. Not even the prison governors are allowed to know who it is they hold. But, while it amuses me to play games with this ignorant youth, and might just possibly yield me some advantage, I would not lie to the future. I *am* Danton. It is I who will die this sixteenth day of Germinal in the Year Two. True, they like to pretend the trial has not concluded. But we know better. (*He takes out his watch, studies it.*) So. We have a few hours.

(HENRY *returns with card table and stool, lays them down, sets the tray on the table, approaches the Cage, gestures the PRISONER away from the gate with his musket, keys it open, fastens a long chain to the bars, beckons the PRISONER forward, snaps the chain onto his ankle, indicates the tray, heads off down the room again.*) The letter . . . ?

HENRY: (*Leaving*) Eat.

(The PRISONER *ponders, then moves towards the food. Discovers the chain holds him a tantalizing metre or so away from it.*)

PRISONER: Who would be an optimist? (*Bellowing down room.*)

What, is the trial ended, and the sentence death by
starving, doughface?
(HENRY *returns, bowl, razor, metal mirror and towel on a tray
in his hands. Sees the problem. Adjusts stool and table.*)
HENRY: Stay calm, citizen. That's eighty sous . . .
(*The* PRISONER *pays him, surveys the meal, sniffs the wine.*
HENRY *takes out a flask from his pocket, places it on the
table.*)
On the house.
(*The* PRISONER *sniffs it, swigs, swigs again, shakes his
head.*)
PRISONER: Jesus God. Weasel piss.
HENRY: Spanish brandy. All there is. Have you slept?
PRISONER: I don't know.
(*He stuffs food into his mouth without relish.* HENRY *lights a
clay pipe, taps his finger on the water bowl.*)
PRISONER: (*Seeing the toiletries*) Ah.
HENRY: Fifteen sous.
(*The* PRISONER *counts out coins, inspects tray.*)
PRISONER: Soap?
HENRY: (*From pocket*) Five.
PRISONER: We'll make a rich man of ye yet, boy.
(*Thumbs razor, sets metal mirror, begins lathering up.* HENRY
puffs on his pipe, slyly eyes him, drawn to the man.)
PRISONER: Did ye speak with your Gate Serjeant?
HENRY: I did.
(*Silence.*)
PRISONER: Yes?
HENRY: He's opened a book.
PRISONER: A book?
HENRY: On which of us is holding the real You. Us or the
Conciergerie.
PRISONER: Has he?
HENRY: He has you clear favourite.
PRISONER: The letter, Henry. Do ye have his price?
HENRY: A hundred. He says I should ask the same . . .
PRISONER: He has a reliable carrier, yes?

HENRY: He has a fair few, he's thinking to use the Three O'Clock Runner, he has a set deal worked out wi' most o' the Committee Runners . . .

PRISONER: Henry, I said reliable, if he runs for the Committee he'll be a spy for 'em too . . .

HENRY: O'course he's a spy, why should that get in his way, he can't live on wages no more than the rest of us.
(*Long pause. The* PRISONER *nods, takes out a draw-purse, lays coins on the table.*)
But . . .

PRISONER: All right. His. (*Removes gold wedding-band.*) Yours. Worth three, a year from now, five maybe. (*Takes out a letter, lays it on the table.*) But?

HENRY: But he thinks ye're 'im. Says it's too risky.

PRISONER: An innocent document, he can read it, read it yourself, Henry . . .

HENRY: He says it could be in code, calling for a rising of your followers . . .

PRISONER: I have no followers, Henry, it's Danton has the followers, he's a huge man, big swaggerbelly, great arse, broken nose, scar on the lip, a Titan, Hero of the Republic written in blood all over him, *that's* your Danton, friend. I'm the former actor detained in a home for the temporarily cracked and currently on loan to the Luxembourg. I'm the Madman.

HENRY: Are you?

PRISONER: (*Quietly*) You know I am.

HENRY: I know nothing.
(*Silence, eyes, locking.*)

PRISONER: I believe you.

HENRY: You could be anyone.

PRISONER: That's what actors *do*, Henry.

HENRY: What?

PRISONER: *Be.* Anyone. (*Silence. He reaches forward, slides the ring to join the coins, lays his watch on* HENRY's *side.*) Ye know what that's worth?

HENRY: D'ye know what they'll do if we're found? Carrying letters from Him?

4

PRISONER: Trust me, Henry. Ye won't be. It's true I have
trouble on occasions knowing who I am, I'm always clear
about who I'm not. Ye're in no danger. Read.
(HENRY *takes the letter, stares hard at it for a long time. The*
PRISONER *resumes shaving.*)

HENRY: (*Laying it down*) I haven't much reading. Ye'll have to do
it.
(*The* PRISONER *stares at him, smiles at the absence of irony,*
gathers the letter. HENRY *walks round the table, to watch over*
his shoulder.

PRISONER: (*Reads*) 'My dearest wife, I am transferred to the
Luxembourg Prison overnight, where I am held in solitary
confinement the whole time. Send money and succour post-
haste, my condition worsens and I begin to entertain the
morbid fear I may never be restored to freedom. Care for my
sons, won't ye? I miss them so. And know I shall love you
always, on whatever side of the grave. Eternally your
Husband.'

HENRY: That's it?

PRISONER: That's it.

HENRY: What's that on the back?

PRISONER: (*Turns the page*) Ah yes. 'Post scriptum. I have again
petitioned the authorities to allow me to address a company
of active citizens of their choosing to judge the condition of
my mind and determine the question of my sanity. If ye will,
a kind of *convention* of my peers . . . '
(*Shot of the* PRISONER'*s face in the metal shaving mirror,*
staring at his reflection. Bleed in stormy sounds of a packed
Convention Hall.
Fast black.
Up at once. The PRISONER *stands at a high podium in a bright*
downlight staring out, waits for the presidential gavel to
command order.)
(*Echoic; intense in the silence*) . . . Fellow members of the
convention, trusted representatives of the sovereign people,
fathers of this proud republic, friends . . . I do not appear
before you because I fear for my neck. If I had feared for my

neck, my friends, I should have slipped across a border and saved it. I am here before you because I fear for my country. And you cannot take your country with you on the soles of your shoes . . . You will have read by now the contemptible calumnies those terrified midgets of the Committee like to call the charges against me . . . corruption, malfeasance, conspiracy with foreign plotters, secret links with the monarchists, using the public purse to stuff my own, uncivic lack of Virtue . . . all the ancient phantasms of rancid and envious minds dumped unevidenced like so much horseshit upon the floor of the Tribunal to steam and stink me to the Block. Well, you'll forgive me for not fouling my hands with it, gentlemen, for in Germinal Year Two, I must tell you, the chasm opened up between charge and crime has come so wide we are in danger, all of us, of falling into the void. The charges these days are always and only a distraction, deliberately drawn up to deflect us from the culprit's real crime . . . I therefore come before you not to save my life by answering charges but to save my country by confessing my crime.

(*The hall, never seen, grows stormy, some clapping, hostile shouts, gavelling. He waits.*)

And what is that crime? A crime the Committee does not name, a crime that appears nowhere in the continents of statute and decree you have laboured over nor is anywhere known to common law? The crime, gentlemen . . .

(*Outbursts, never lost, well up again above the gavel*) . . .

The crime I freely admit to . . .

(*Hall acoustic dies. Light from below displaces the downspot. His eyes take the lens; hold the stare.*)

(*Voice over; inward, grave*) You have given me such a hatred for the present, I find myself longing for the days when the whole of my weekly income depended on a bottle of ink . . . You have filled me with such fear for the future, I spend my last hours rehearsing what will not happen as though it were already history. So much rising to be said, underneath, so much to hold down, so much to bite back, or choke on. How will I tell you what matters? How will I tell you, as I scan

6

your tiny faces in the gloom, you are yourselves already dead,
immured inside the dungeon walls of cant and lies and
language this revolution has all the while and under our noses
been a-building? How will I tell you I am grown mild? How
will I tell you: it is April . . . ?
(*Angle. Light change. He sits as before, letter before him,* HENRY
gazing at it over his shoulder.)
(*Reads*) '. . . But whatever happens, do not let Paré neglect
Tiger, who needs regular exercise, so let him begin tomorrow
and every day until I'm home and can do it for myself.'
(*Silence. The* PRISONER *splashes his face with water, dries it on
the towel. Looks up at* HENRY.)
Satisfied?

HENRY: (*Finger poking envelope*) S'that say?
PRISONER: Mme Louise Gèly, 22 Rue de Commerce, Cordeliers.
HENRY: (*Poking letter*) S'that say?
PRISONER: Freedom.
HENRY: That?
PRISONER: Grave.
HENRY: Who's Tiger?
PRISONER: The dog.
HENRY: Sounds more like a cat, Tiger.
PRISONER: He's a dog.
HENRY: Does he look like a tiger?
PRISONER: Why would he? He's a dog.
HENRY: Who's Paré?
    (*Silence.*)
PRISONER: My valet. Or, in the language of the new political
    correctitude, 'house assistant'. Now, what could be more
    innocent? Trust me.
    (HENRY *gathers the letter in his fingertips, rounds the card table,
    lays it down between the watch and the coins and ring.*)
HENRY: The thing is.
PRISONER: Go on.
HENRY: I've an infirm mother and nine young brothers and
    sisters to keep fed. If I'm found . . . Even if you're not Him
    . . . (*Shrugs. Shakes his head.*)

7

PRISONER: It's a gamble. I see that. (*Uncaps flask, takes a pull on it.*) The watch is worth six hundred livres, the ring's solid gold. What do they pay you?

HENRY: Three livres a day.

PRISONER: I'd be tempted.

HENRY: Would you?

PRISONER: I would.

HENRY: I am.

PRISONER: You should be. (*He raises the brandy flask, glugs for a moment, suddenly spumes a mouthful of it into the air, showering his upturned face in the downpour. Words form in his throat.*) Germ. Germinate. Germinal. April. Growing weather.

HENRY: (*Recoiling; musket ready*) Eh eh eh. Don't start that.

PRISONER: It's out of my hands, friend. It's why I'm detained. Will you do it?
(HENRY *picks up the watch, puts it to his ear, smells it. Fingers the letter. Heavy sifting rain has begun outside, drizzling the blue-walled Salle with rain shadow.*)

HENRY: (*Delivered as one thought*) I wouldn't get 'em through, there's thirteen doors between here and the Gate House, every one of 'em under special guard for as long as you're held here, I'm searched coming and going, they find this I lose my certificate of civic worthiness at the very least, I paid good bribe money for that, and no certificate, no job, I wouldn't get 'em through . . .
(*The* PRISONER *takes the letter, delicately winds it into a roll, leans carefully forward to place it in the barrel of the guard's musket. Smiles.*)

PRISONER: Our lives are much like the theatre, Henry, indifferently written and scandalously short of rehearsal. Like poor actors, we must learn to trust one another. And be bold together. Henry . . .

HENRY: What if they look ins –

PRISONER: They won't. Would *you*?

HENRY: No. But *if*.

PRISONER: Your finger slips on the trigger. Pouf, up in smoke. (*Silence.*)

8

HENRY: If you *are* the Madman . . .

PRISONER: If?

HENRY: . . . how come you have all the answers?
(*Silence.*)

PRISONER: If I have all the answers, friend, what the fuck am I
doing here . . . ? (*He gestures the Cage, the prison, the world.
Puts his chained foot up on the stool.*) Come on, do what ye
will, I've had enough . . .
(HENRY *finds the key, warily releases him, follows as the*
PRISONER *returns to the Cage, begins to relock the door on him,
sees the casually palmed bottle from the table in the* PRISONER's
*hand, gently dispossesses him of it, locks the door. Dwells a
moment. Watches the* PRISONER *squat in the straw, head in
hands, morose, inturned.*)

HENRY: I promise nothing. I'll give it thought.

PRISONER: (*Not looking*) Who shall be happy . . . ? *What?* Be
happy *what?*
(*Silence.*)

HENRY: Sleep. (*Moves to the table, collects musket and tray, stares
hard at coins, ring, watch, confronted by them.
Silence.*)

PRISONER: Take. Get the feel of it in your pocket.
(HENRY's *face, taut with the problem.
*PRISONER's *face, watching intently. His point of view, through
bars, of* HENRY's *hands finally pocketing the loot.
Downshot of* PRISONER *through roof-bars, head still bowed,
neck bared. He turns his head to follow the guard's lumpy
departure down the Salle.
On the tilt,* HENRY *reaches doors, knocks before unlocking them,
stands framed in doorway to be searched, finally turns to close
and relock doors.
The* PRISONER's *head jerks upwards, as the slam echoes around
the room. His eyes find the overhead lens. He smiles. Holds up
the filched cut-throat, blade a dull glint.*)
I play this game for hope. And know I must hold myself
ready for the worst. The *big* one we call the *National* Razor.
Sometimes, the Hot Hand.

9

(*He stares hard at the blade. Folds and pockets it. Town clock
sounds the half. Thunder.*
*He fumbles in his greatcoat pocket, comes up with a short fipple-
flute.*
*Wide deep shot of the room, the Cage. He begins to play: a
slowed-down, haunting verse or two of 'Ça Ira', the Republic's
favourite carillon.*
Cuts abruptly, mid-phrase.)
Tiger's code for the people. As in: if you would master a
revolution, first you must learn to ride the Tiger. If the
letter's carried, she will know what to do. Let the Tiger stir
tomorrow, Danton may yet come whole from this.
(*Chuckles.*) Picture it. A rising at the courtroom, the old
sections armed and marching again, the folk of '89 and '91,
the folk of August '92, June '93, the plain people, menu
people we call 'em, whose only wish is to be included in the
fucking meal . . . Or in the Square itself, *real* drama, a
legendary last-minute snatch from the block . . . Ah. The
very stuff of story-time. (*Dwells.*) It won't happen. The odds
are all the other way. I play this game for hope; without it,
what are we if not already dead? In these few years, in this
unlikely place, these people have lived and fought and died
to claim hope for the human project, to make hope the
inalienable right of the living. They have decreed it: to hope
is to be human; to hope is to define ourselves as human.
Nobody can change that now; it will be so, part of the
condition. Like me tonight, you too cannot live but in hope.
Liberty may wither, Fraternity evaporate, Equality rot on
the vine, Hope's a survivor; and will not die. (*He looks
around him: Cage, Salle, world. Bellows.*) Long live the Free
Republic! Long live the men and women who made her!
Long live Danton . . . who did what he could!
(*The cries echo round the vast chamber, meld with the sudden
rolling thunder, die. He chuckles.*)
A world of space to fill with words and not a soul to hear.
Never mind. We have our roles and it's enough. Storytime.
Where were we? We need some colour, I think, mm? Some

people . . . who d'ye want? I can give ye a whole gallery of folk.
You want Marat? (*He muzzes his hair, deranges his shirt, grows
short, Italian, scrofulous, operatically intense; utterly
transformed.*) Marat you shall have . . . 'Friends, fellow
Jacobins. Do not be deceived when they tell you things are
better now. Even if there is no poverty to be seen because the
poverty's been hidden. Even if you ever got more wages and
could afford to buy more of these new and useless goods which
industries foist on you and even if it seems to you you've never
had so much, that is only the slogan of those who still have
much more than you. Do not be taken in when they pat you on
the shoulder and say there's no inequality worth speaking of
and no more reason to fight, because if you believe them they
will be completely in charge in their marble homes and granite
banks, from which they rob the peoples of the world under the
pretence of bringing them enlightenment. Watch out, my
friends, for as soon as it pleases them they'll be sending you
out to protect their gold in wars whose weapons, rapidly
developed by servile Science, will become more and more
deadly until they can, with a flick of the finger, tear a million of
you to pieces . . .'
(*Silence*)
Dear Jean-Paul. The Apostle of Liberty, Friend of the
People, Seer of the Republic and everybody's favourite
lunatic. Met him first in '86, '87, in bed, as it happens, in a
rather recherché brothel owned by Orléans, the King's cousin
and Prince of the Blood. I was busy excavating the daughter of
the Comtesse de Saint-Amaranthe who ran it, while the
Comtesse lay beside us having her motte truffled. By, as it
turned out, the aforesaid Friend of the People. Not a lot
passed between us on that occasion. I may have introduced
myself *en passant*. I believe he moaned a time or two, perhaps
his name, I'm not sure. Back then he called himself de Mara, a
blue blood, full wig, powder, perfume, face paint, breeched
and buckled, as befits a man who had quacked himself into a
lucrative practice as doctor to the nobility while shafting half
the wives of fashionable Paris . . . Those were the days.

II

(*Silence.*
He dwells on the man; sombre.) On, on. More colour, more
life, more *people*. Who? Say it, say it. Ah . . . (*He fiddles a wig*
from his pocket, fastidiously reorganizes his dress, grows eerily
priest-like, precise, precious, fashions a nosegay from straw to
ward off the stench of humanity.) Yes, of course . . . Who else?
. . . Maxim the Incorruptible, Maximillion Miseries . . .
'What is the purpose of the Terror under revolutionary
government? I will tell you. It is to create the Republic. Not
just by the word of statute but by the deed of action. The aim
of constitutional government is to preserve the Republic.
The aim of revolutionary government is to found it. In the
teeth of its murderous liberticide enemies, both abroad and
within. Under revolutionary rule, the public power has the
duty to defend itself against all the factions that attack it. For
it has become clear, midway through Year Two of our
Republic, that faction itself is grown the chief threat to our
work, faction that fattens on two deviations: weakness and
rashness, moderatism and excess. Moderatism which is to
moderation as impotence is to chastity. Excess which is to
vigour as dropsy is to health. But let it be understood. These
factions, these enemies of the Republic, have great
advantages, since on their side lie all the vices, while the
Republic has only humble virtues to call on in its defence.
Virtues are simple, modest, poor, often ignorant, sometimes
gross. Vices are surrounded by riches, carouse in the arms of
pleasure and debauch in the halls of perfidy; they are the
companions of all the dangerous talents; they are constantly
escorted by crime. They gnaw all about us; they take our
brothers by surprise; they caress our passions; seek to sway
our opinions . . .'
(*Silence.*
He stops, tunnelled, turned in; eventually removes the wig, barely
aware he does it. Little more than whispered)
The man who has decided I must die.
The man who would be certain.
Who has outlawed doubt. Doubleness.

All blur, haze and hover.
Wrote. One year ago. A day or so
After.
After.
My Gabrielle. Birthing a dead daughter.
Died . . . .
(*Silence.*)
. . . And I had,
Detained in Belgium.
Back too late. Dug up
Her corpse
To gaze on her a
Last dead
Time . . .
(*Silence.*)
Wrote. A year ago. The same man.
A propos. (*Own voice, but the man's wig in his hand.*)
'If, amidst the only misfortunes capable of shaking a soul
like thine, the certainty of having a tender and devoted
friend may bring thee some consolation, I offer that to thee.
I love thee better than ever; and till death. From this
moment forward I am thee. Close not thy heart to the
words of an affection that shares all thy suffering. Let us
weep together for the dear friend you have lost. I should
have come to see thee, had I not respected the first
moments of thy legitimate affliction. Embrace thy friend.
Robespierre.'
(*Silence, save for the rain. He shivers, draws up his collar. Takes
out the cut-throat. Opens it. Stares at it.*)
(*Voice over:*) I could never embrace him. Who have hugged
hundreds. How do you embrace a vapour, an incorporeal
idea . . .? A system on legs . . . ? (*He rises, carries the blade to
the Cage door, stoops to work on the lock. Talks as he works.*)
Come and speak with me, my 'friend till death'. I know
you're not sleeping, up there in your virtuous cot. I hear
you've been sick again. But who hasn't? You'll find me much
as I always was, still seeking to extend the range of human

possibilities . . . (*Click. He stops, stands, smiles. Lays a finger's weight on the Cage door. The door truckles a few decisive inches outwards. He fingers it slowly open.*) One road to freedom opened. (*Stares out into the blackness. Lays the blade to his larynx.*) And here's another.

(*Close shot: mouth, chin, neck, blade. The neck's nicked: bright beads of blood begin a slow slither down the throat.*
A rip of lightning, another, across the image. Thunder, close, serious.)

PRISONER'S VOICE/PRISONER (*Alternating*): April

Who . . .

How will I tell them?

Shall . . .

Seedtime, Louise

Be . . .

Ah

Happy . . . ?

Yes.

. . . Happy *what* . . . ?

(*Hard, urgent*) Yes yes. My girl bride.

Who shall be happy . . . *what*?

(*Smash cut to: mute point of view: spring sky, Arcis-sur-Aube; a circle of trees joined at the canopy.*
On reverse, the PRISONER, *on his back on a mossed bank, drying in the sun.*
Bleed in birds, insects, country; then nearby swimming sounds. Someone leaves the water. He shifts to watch: his eyes chart the approach. A shadow falls across his face.
His point of view: directly above him, naked, glistening, his new wife LOUISE, *almost sixteen, the pond beyond. The blocked sun silvers her outline, blackens the rest: unreal.*)

PRISONER: What?

LOUISE'S VOICE: Wet.

PRISONER: Yet?

(*She gestures him to feel. His hand moves gently up between her spread thighs. The fingers reach her, slowly sink into the black.*)

LOUISE'S VOICE: Again.

(*She moans, moves on her heels. He sits up to lay his face at her
lower belly. Her hands draw him in.*)
Now.
PRISONER: How?
(*Smash cut to: close shot of their bodies, locked, fierce, thrashing
the pond in the roll, suck and plunder of the fuck. Calls, cries,
mutters thrill up into the darkening canopy, the sun half-gone.*)
(*Voice over*): Kissing a son on the mouth. Knowing my
mother eats. Horse sweat. Cheesecake and cider at the
Procope. Wood-smoke. Swimming in the Seine. My new
bride's sweet cunt in my nostrils all day. Frost. Men's
laughter.
(*Flesh melds, almost there; film slows, bleaches.*)
(*Voice over; a whisper:*) Oh Robespierre, my 'friend till
death', what will *you* miss, when your turn comes . . .? The
Committee? The Podium? The Terror? The Instruments of
Rule? How sad to leave this earth so . . . untouched by it.
How sad the man who has never embraced commonness,
who has not dared to be ordinary . . .
(*The slowed bleached image blurs. 'Ça Ira' again: fipple-flute.
Slow mix through to wide shot of the room, the open untenanted
Cage. Fipple-flute continues, somewhere in the dark.
The shot begins a calm, wheeling search of the great Salle: finds
an ancient discomfited armchair, a leg missing; rubble, lumber, a
shattered chandelier, scraps of earlier meanings.*)
PRISONER'S VOICE: **Who** . . .
The future lies in an alley, its throat slit . . .
Shall . . .
Even as we have been new-minting the coins of hope . . .
Be . . .
We have been yet busier reissuing the banknotes of despair . . .
Happy . . .?
Twin legacies bequeathed on all who come after . . .
If . . .
(*Music cuts. The shot has found him. He squats beneath the
table, fipple-flute in hands, trembling.*)
If. *If.* Who shall be happy if . . .? (*Can't find the rest. Roars,*

anguished.) WHO SHALL BE HAPPY IF *WHAT*? WHAT?
(*The roar jags around the space. The shot follows it: ceilings, plasterwork, shuttered windows; the search resumed.*
Out of shot, echoic, somewhere in the room, singing)
> A hero is honoured no longer
> Than it pays to have him about
> We reap the fruits of his labour
> And then we sling him out.
> This may not seem fair play
> But that's the people's way
> In a Re Re Re
> In a pub pub pub
> In a Re-a pub-a Republic.

(*The shot's found him; closes in on the skewed armchair he sits in. A town clock sounds the quarter.*)
The song that toppled a king. August '92, the Champs de Mars again, this time we meant business, this time we would remake the world. Reinvent it. Year One of the Free Republic. There was even a play included it on stage, sung by 'Danton' himself. Commissioned especially by the Cordeliers district to mark the Champs de Mars rising and their leading figure's leading role in it. My friend D'Eglantine wrote some of it, I believe, a group of local actors the rest. The plan was to present it at the next Festival of the Nation . . . But it fell foul of the authorities. Never actually performed. There seemed to have been a widespread feeling that the title had something to do with its neglect – 'Danton Saves France' – I can't think why. Never mind. There'll be others.
(*The shot moves on, continues the calm wheeling search across the dark silent spaces.*)
(*Out of shot, echoic*)
> With a Dan Dan Dan
> With a Ton Ton Ton
> With a dear old, damned old Danton.

(*The shot finds him leaning face forward against the Salle doors. Sounds as of a running tap.*

Finding lens) Historians of a sentimental cast may want to read this as that deep desire in all of us to say 'Hello, well met' to those we cannot otherwise touch . . .
(*He turns his face back to the door, slides the grille-cover very gently open. Guards sprawl in the passageway, sleeping. He looks down towards his feet. Close shot of his urine streaming down and under the doors, headed for the sleeping men. Faint sounds of snoring from the guards on the other side.*)
(*Out of shot*) The rest of you will know better.
(*The snoring falters, as if disturbed; stalls; pecks on.*)
(*Out of shot*) The letter's already history. Ça ira. It's not . . .
(*Mixing through to: Cage. He's stooped inside the door, relocking it with the razor.*)
. . . escape I seek.
It's rescue.
It's not life I ask.
It's meaning.
(*Mixing through to: wide shot of the Cage, the man laid out motionless on the divan within.*
Cut to: slow overhead track up the prone PRISONER, *foot to face. Dwells at the top of the knee-boots; the metal knob of the cut-throat glints there, slid between leg and leather. Moves on up the body, over hands crossed at breast, greatcoat buttoned to top. To face. It's white, still, as if embalmed; eyes closed.*
Town clock strikes: four. Prison noises, faint, approaching. The eyes open.
Fists at the doors, raised voices. He sits up; becomes aware of HENRY *at the table, playing Patience.*
More fists. HENRY *mutters, gathers his gun, trudges down the room. The* PRISONER *watches, listens. Fragments of what's said drift up to the Cage from the gloom.*
HENRY: . . . The prisoner is safe and under watch, Captain.
VOICE: Stay at yer post, understood?
(*More talk, instructions. From other parts of the huge building, the din of search parties – whistles, bells, dogs, boots – begins to feed in to the Salle.*
HENRY *lumbers back to the table, props up his musket, returns to*

his cards, his back to the Cage. Notices his boots are wet. Stoops, sniffs.)

HENRY: Dirty buggers. They'd piss in their own bed, some folk . . .

(The PRISONER *stands, pads over to the bars, watches.)*

PRISONER: *(Soft)* Knave.

HENRY: *(Swivelling)* What . . .? Awake, are ye?

PRISONER: S'the clock?

*(*HENRY *consults the* PRISONER'S *watch at his waist.)*

HENRY: *(Eventually)* Four. *(Lips counting.)* Seven after. *(Turns back to his cards, studies them.)*

PRISONER: Knave to queen to king.

(Shot of the cards. HENRY'S *hand lifts the jack to the vacant queen and all to the king.)*

HENRY: How'd ye do that? Ye got a glass in there ?

PRISONER: Party trick. Sometimes it works.

*(*HENRY *shakes his head, resumes the game. Search sounds persist, at distance.)*

What's the commotion?

HENRY: *(At play)* S'nothin'. The usual bollox. The Committee have uncovered another plot. National Guard are sent in to foil it. Hundreds o' the buggers. *(Begins untying a kerchiefed bundle.)* Ye hungry? I'm havin' me snap while I can. *(He turns, takes in the man's headshake.)* Ye all right? Ye look like death in a dustbin . . . *(He surveys the snap: black bread, a knot of cheese, a green potato, a pinch or two of oats. Pours a dab of brandy on the oats, works it in, tries it.)* A prison rising, they reckon. A Royalist gang under General Dillon, planning to kill the guards, spring the Man-in-Question and set him up king or someat. S'what I'm told, anyroad.

PRISONER: Mm. Good to know the Committee's not lost its talent for comedy. So this rising . . .

HENRY: *(Focus on cards)* There's no rising. This place were like a graveyard till they came. Happens a lot. A week or two back, it were a plot to spring old whatsisname and the Commune crowd, none of it ever comes to aught . . .

PRISONER: Hèbert . . . ?

18

HENRY: Aye, that's him. Gate Serjeant reckons they only do it to keep our toes on the line.
(*He plays on. The* PRISONER *peels back from the bars, sits on the divan, head down, his gaze on the floor between his feet.*)
Ye don't ask if I took the letter through.

PRISONER: No.

HENRY: Well I did.

PRISONER: I hoped ye would.

HENRY: Cackin' mesen I were. Thought I'd never mek it to that Gate House. But I did.
(*Silence. The* PRISONER *looks across at* HENRY, *deep in the game.*)

PRISONER: And is it sent?

HENRY: Sent? Not yet. It's waiting a carrier.
(*Silence.*)

PRISONER: I thought ye were to use the Committee's man . . .

HENRY: The Three O'Clock Runner? Ruled out. He's nailed here till mornin', waiting on the Governor to finish the search and report all's safe. We've had to look elsewhere.
(*Silence. The* PRISONER'*s head goes down again.* HENRY *stands, lights his pipe, ambles over to the Cage.*)
It'll be took. Hard part's behind us. I've a cousin works in the kitchens, he's off at five and ready to carry it . . . Asks a hundred, he'll settle for half.
(*The* PRISONER *looks up at him, eyes sunk, face pale, drawn.*)

PRISONER: Ye took the purse, Henry, that's all I had.

HENRY: Mm. No valuables, pieces? (*The man shakes his head.*)
What's the coat worth?

PRISONER: The coat?

HENRY: (*Studying it*) He'd tek the coat.
(*Long silence.*)
I shall need to send word 'fore five. To say if he's to tek the letter or not . . .
(*The* PRISONER'*s hand moves up to the collar-buttons.*)
Keep it on. Do later.
(HENRY *watches on a moment, drawn but wary. The man stares on at the floor.*

HENRY *ambles back to the table, angles his seat to take in the Cage, relights his pipe, returns to his cards.*)

PRISONER: (*From nowhere*) I was with my wife earlier. I was lying with Gabrielle, the night the first-born died. But it was she was the quick one, me the dead. Yet I could smell her tears on the pillow. The lavender she kept beneath.

HENRY: Dreams be weird.

(*The man produces the fipple-flute. Plays 'Ça Ira', low, slow, perfect.* HENRY *listens, wholly drawn. He finishes. Stares at the flute, his fingers hovering over the stops.*)

HENRY: Will ye come out for a spell?

PRISONER: (*Slowly*) If ye like.

HENRY: Ye calm?

PRISONER: Aye.

HENRY: (*The chain*) Put that on. I've a bottle somewhere.

(*He heads down the room, finds his knapsack, draws a bottle of wine from it, finds a couple of battered tin cups, returns to the table, crosses to unlock the Cage door. The* PRISONER *waits, chain at ankle,* HENRY *checks it's secured, lets him through to the table.*)

Here. (*A mug.*) We'll tek a drink.

(*He fills the mugs with red. They look at each other.*)

The Republic.

PRISONER: The Republic.

(*They clank, drink, eye each other again as the cups come down.*)

HENRY: (*Decking cards*) Cards 'r chat?

PRISONER: (*Deliberate*) I'm without money, Henry.

HENRY: (*Cards away*) Oh aye. Chat then.

(*Silence. Wine. Distant sounds of search. They look at each other across the smoke and gleam of the guard's lamp.*)

Ye wanna play Last Words?

PRISONER: Last Words of the Blessed Martyrs? By the cankered cock of Christ the Worker, child, why can we not just sit?

HENRY: This un's just called Last Words. It can be anybody. And ye don't 'ave to know what they said, y'ave to mek 'em up. Wanna play?

20

PRISONER: *How*, for God's sake? If there's no true or false,
there's no way of scoring . . .

HENRY: Ye get a point for a laugh. Or a shiver. Or a tear. We
made it up at school. Them as couldn't read.
(*The* PRISONER *stares at him; loves his innocence.*)
Like, you give me Joan of Arc, I say, now ye see me, now ye
don't, that's one I made up, it's not usually that fast . . . You
say the King of England, I say . . . (*He lifts a buttock, issues a
great mouth-fart.*) That's another one . . .
(*Silence. A slow, contained mute laugh begins to build up in the
PRISONER's chest. Splashes of it spray up his frame, to throat, to
voice, mouth.* HENRY *follows, chuckles, pleased. As the laugh
reaches the face, it begins a slow agonizing collapse into pain and
fear and abject misery. Small sounds move about the jaw and
mouth; big in the silence.*
HENRY *waits, watches, trying to read how things are; where.
The spasm ends. The* PRISONER *sits on, as if somewhere else.*
HENRY *pushes the bottle down the table. Touches the man's
elbow with it, coaxing him back.
The man sees the bottle, fills up, drinks.*)
Where there's life, eh?

PRISONER: Aye. (*The* PRISONER *stands, studies the room, as if
seeing it for the first time.*) I'll sleep, I think.

HENRY: Finish your cup. I'll tell ye a story. (*The* PRISONER *sits.*)
Will I? (*The* PRISONER *shrugs.*) It's not a story as such, it's
someat 'appened earlier on at t'Gate House, ye might have a
thought or two on it when it's told . . . Tek your mind off
things?
(*The* PRISONER *shrugs.* HENRY *restocks his pipe bowl, tops up
his cup.*)
Ye'll recall I spoke of the Three O'Clock Runner, he was to
be the carrier for your . . .? (*Takes the man's nod.*) Now,
when I get to the Gate House with the letter in my musket,
my guts are in a turmoil, I wasn't ticklin' ye, I have to hot
heel it to the Necessary or my trousers'll tek the lot . . . Now,
while I'm in there, who's in the next box but Birdie, the
Three O'Clock Runner . . . that's what we call him, Birdie . . .

he has this great . . . *nose* stickin' out of his face like a . . .
tap, like a . . . Bit of a jack-the-lad, oh yes, knows everythin',
misses naught, meks his way . . . So we're squattin' there
next each other, he's just brought the letter in from the
Committee – the plot, right? – he's cursin' an' bubblin' he's
gonna lose private trade because of it, ructions and alarums
are the buggeration o' folk like us, he says . . . So he's lookin'
to make up his losses by laying a decent dollop with the
Serjeant on who's holding the Big Un . . . the Man-in-
Question, see. An' o' course he's pressing me for clues, I
mean he's asking how ye look, how ye talk, what ye say,
what ye wear . . . 'Cos he *knows*, he's been in the same room
as the Man many a time, recent as yesterday he reckons,
down at the Court . . .

(*Silence.* HENRY *relights pipe. The* PRISONER *sips more wine.*)

PRISONER: So. Did ye tell him?

HENRY: Tell him? (*Emphatic.*) No.

(*Faint, pre-dawn birdsong: blackbird.*)

Dull I may be, I'm no fool. He's a starling, is Birdie.
Chatchatchat. He'd clean the Gate Serjeant out and brag how
he did it all across town, can't help it, chatchatchat . . .
Serjeant gets to know an' I'm *brawn*, mister. Not a man to
cross, our Gate Serjeant.

(*Silence.* HENRY *broods. The* PRISONER *takes a look. Stands
again.*)

PRISONER: Is it over?

HENRY: What?

PRISONER: The story.

HENRY: Nearly. There's a bit more.

(*The* PRISONER *sits. Search sounds drift in: shouts, barks.*)

I cross the yard back to the Gate House. National Guard're
still pourin' in, droves of 'em, tryin' a form lines in two
hands o' water, the Under-Governor's out, helpin' the
officers with the list o' suspects, it's time I were back 'ere, I
say, better safe than sorry . . . I'm passing through the Gate
House, on my way, big old stable it were once, I see this
feller at the other end warming his arse at t'stove an' holding

22

forth, I say I know that feller, I come a bit closer, I see it's
the Three O'Clock Runner. (*Long hold.*) An' that's very
strange, because . . . when I first seen him I'd been minded
o' someone else altogether.

PRISONER: (*Slow*) Ye lose me, lad.

HENRY: Hold on. Ye'll catch up. Now I could *hear*, I knew at
once what were goin' on, he were tellin' a *story*, see, an'
every now an' then he'd . . . do . . . be . . . someone in the
story, someone else. Remember, ye said it yesen earlier on,
'bout acting, *bein' anyone*, remember?
(*The* PRISONER *flicks a look, eyes hooded.*)
He was tellin' 'em about bein' down at the Tribunal
building yesterday, waitin' on a package or someat . . . and
poppin' in to t'courtroom to watch t'trial . . . So like he's
the judge one minute, then he's the prosecutor, he's a
defendant, he's someone in t'crowd callin' someat . . . Now
ye see him, now ye don't, eh? . . . (*Grins.*) Then he's back
to t'first feller. The one as took my eye. And it's Danton.
The Man himself. (*He stands, swells a little, going for the
gesture.*) An' he's *goin'* at the fuckers, like a bull, head down
an' both horns shinin' . . . 'Call this *justice*, ye dribbling sack
o' snot, ye festering pot o' pig's piss, just remember, those
who drink the people's blood die of it . . . You call my
witnesses, all seventeen of 'em, for tomorrow, or this
pantomime can continue without me, I refuse my
consent . . .'
(*He resumes his stool, looks across at the* PRISONER.)
. . . Birdie does it better than me, o' course . . .

PRISONER: (*A nod*) Do more. What else did he say?

HENRY: What else? I don't know. I had to bring mysen back
'ere 'fore the searching parties set up. (*Thinks.*) Wasn't what
he *said* as mattered. It were who he were . . . bein', when he
said it . . .

PRISONER: (*Slow*) I thought ye said he was . . . being Danton,
am I wrong . . . ?

HENRY: (*Looking at him*) Danton. Right.
(*Silence.*)

23

PRISONER: Well. However long ye live, Henry, it's unlikely ye'll ever get closer to the Man. Poor sod.
(*He stands, drinks up, waits, wanders to the Cage, sits on the divan, stares back at the watching* HENRY. *Shakes the chain on his ankle.*)
If ye've a minute, friend . . .
(*Begins removing his greatcoat.* HENRY *slings his musket, approaches with his keys. Stoops to unshackle him. For a moment, in close shot, the cut-throat at the top of the knee-boot sits, undetected, in his immediate eye-line.*)

HENRY: Thing is. It wasn't . . . Danton . . . I was minded of. Because. I don't know Danton, never met, never seen him . . . It wasn't Danton Birdie was . . . bein'. For me. Couldn'ta bin.
(*The town clock strikes the half.*)

PRISONER: (*Handing him the coat*) Makes sense. Ye'll not forget to send word to your cousin . . .

HENRY: (*Simply*) It was you. Everything. Voice and walk and head and . . . everything. (*He stands, folds the coat for carrying, drags the chain to the doorway, lays it down.*) I tell ye, I'd never play Last Words wi' the Three O'Clock Runner. He can make ye shiver . . . Anyroad. That's the story.
(*Turns, looks at him.*) Any thoughts? Now it's told.

PRISONER: (*Still*) Henry. Leave me be. (*He drags his legs onto the litter, lies back, closes his eyes. Quiet, metallic.*) I cannot speak on this. Too. Painful. Too. Riving. It will make me weep again. And my tears will drown the world. Do not ask. I've cracked enough. More and I will break.
(HENRY *waits. Closes door.*)

HENRY: I hear ye. (*Thinks.*) Mister, I've tried to be honest with ye, I'll not alter now . . . I'll not let my cousin take that letter, not from Him . . . you. (*He turns the key in the lock.*) Not now I know what I know. There it is.
(*He holds on a moment or two, turns to clump back to the table. The* PRISONER *remains motionless.*
Close tightening shot of his face, neck, blood caked below the nick. Bring up:)

(*Voice over, reprised*) Call this *justice*, ye dribbling sack o'
snot, ye festering pot o' pig's piss, just remember, those who
drink the people's blood die of it . . .
(*The image behind his closed eyelids has displaced the shot of the
face. It's bleached, half-speed, mute: a tightening point of view
from distance of the* THREE O'CLOCK RUNNER *at the Gate
House stove doing his Danton in the dock.*)
(*Voice over*) You. Everything. Voice and walk and head and
. . . everything.
(*The shot has tightened to close-up of the* RUNNER'*s face. We
recognize the* PRISONER.
Moving back to: close shot, PRISONER'*s face, in Cage as before.
The eyes open: they're calm, rational, dealing with the problem.*
HENRY'*s resumed his seat at the table, his back once more to the
cage.*
The PRISONER *sits up sharply, feet to floor, hand for a hovering
moment at his boot-top. Glares hard at the young* GUARD'*s back.
Stands. Shifts to better light. Finds the declamatory stance.
Launches.*)

PRISONER: (*Big; as actor*) . . . Citizens, patriots, builders and
shakers of the world's good morrow, you are welcome here.
The New Theatre for the Old Cordeliers is proud and
privileged to offer you this evening an entirely novel piece –
the work principally of the celebrated revolutionary and poet
Fabre d'Eglantine, with additional scenes by members of the
company (*indicates them behind him*), which we respectfully
entitle *Danton Saves France* . . .
(*Sound fades abruptly as he continues the 'speech', displaced by:*)
(*Voice over*) There be times we must strut and stamp and
shake our whores' heads, though dignity and self-esteem
deem it beneath us . . . We play the game to win or not at all.
(*Fade back up to:*)
(*Voice over ends*) . . . There falls to me, dear friends, the
enduring honour, the impossible task, of seeking to fill the
boots of our eponymous hero . . . Yes, my friends, like a
small boy reaching for the Pole Star, I must essay for the
evening . . . the Man Himself. (*Shifts voice.*) Applause

25

applause applause, company leave stage left, climb onto
the rostrum (*steps up onto divan*), find the light . . . (*As
Danton again*) Greetings, friends and fellow citizens.
Name's Danton, for those who don't know me. Born and
reared in the country, the Champagne, but not the sleek
rolling part, the scrawny bit . . . of common stock, decent
honest toilers, living useful lives in uncelebrated places,
dying obscurely as if they had never lived . . . So expect
no charms and graces, I am as I come . . .
(*Shot of* HENRY *face on, listening, the Cage and* PRISONER
behind him, back of shot.)
. . . But come, friends, come and see for yourselves. To
my village, to our plain family house, to our life some
thirty years and several millennia ago, in the reign of the
fifteenth Louis – Louis the Penultimate, as I prefer to call
him – when the world and I were young . . .
(*Close profile shot of* PRISONER, HENRY *back of shot. Sound
fades abruptly on the still-performing 'Danton', displaced by:*)
(*Voice over*) . . . I will turn this boy, I will not let him be
the death of me, I will win him to my purpose, I will turn
him, he will not immure me inside the bastille of his
ignorance, I will touch his soul, he will turn . . .
(*Fade back up the continuing 'speech':* PRISONER *foreground,*
HENRY *back.*)
. . . Seven years passed, I was ten. But I had not forgotten
that bloody bull and the injuries he had done me. One
day, I took a stout stave and sought him out in his field,
ready to pay him out. The bull was older too; bigger,
fiercer. I waved the stick and waited. (*Very slowly, back of
shot,* HENRY *begins to turn.*) He sees me. Lowers his head.
Charges. (*Silence. A slow grin.*) I awoke some hours later
in my mother's bed, with a broken nose, three cracked
teeth, bruised to buggery and a very important lesson
learnt: A man may do everything save the impossible. It
was not until much later I discovered that only men
together, people together, can do *anything*, possible or
not. . .

26

(*He gives the watching* HENRY *a long look, steps down from the divan, moves to the bars.*)

How will I fetch you to understanding, friend? It is not possible to be Georges-Jacques Danton and not mad. It is possible to be mad but not Danton. Henry . . . Why do you imagine the Committee had *me* put here this night? D'ye think any piece of meat would have served? I *played* him, Henry. In a play. For weeks and months I followed him, watched him, heard him . . . studied how I might become him, the voice and walk and head. Everything. (*Stops.*) So hard to speak of. So hard to . . . (*Stops.*) When you stand. In another's man's boots. Until they seem your own. And your own. No longer fit you . . . Do ye understand any of this, Henry? Ye know what ye know but ye do not know the *truth* and I am powerless to tell ye because my mouth and throat are so . . . filled by it I cannot breathe, it is drowning me . . . (*He takes out the cut-throat, opens it.* HENRY *rises, face pale, impossible to read.*) Henry, were I indeed the Man-in-Question, the Hero of the Republic, the Champion of the Oppressed, the Saviour of the Nation, the Towering Titan of the Revolution, the People's Voice, the Bull among Men, the Fathering Spirit of all the Republics yet to be born into peace and justice and freedom and plenty, were I *that* man, Henry, surely by now I would have slit your insignificant throat and fed you to the rats. (*Silence.*) Instead . . . (*He draws open his collars, baring the blooded neck.* HENRY *stares, eyes unblinking.*) I'll not be free until He's dead and gone. But may not kill Him without I kill myself. Only in death is there freedom: this is the true madness of our time. (*Pause.*) I'm not the Prince, Henry. I'm the frog who swallowed him . . .

(*He folds the cut-throat, stoops, lays it gently down outside the Cage. Draws away from the bars, to give him safe space.*)

I could not harm ye. For you are a good man.

(HENRY *stares at the cut-throat, moves to gather it up; looks up at him from the stoop. The man's eyes are raw, desperate. Silence.*

27

A sudden loud banging at the doors. HENRY *stands, listens. It stops briefly.*)

Henry.

(*The banging sets up again.* HENRY *collects his musket, slogs off down the room. The* PRISONER *follows his progress through the side-bars; sees him slide open the grille-cover to mutter with someone outside; turns; finds the overhead lens.*)

In one month last winter, eight hundred people died of hunger and cold in the district of St Antoine. In all there are forty-eight such districts in the capital. Preponderantly the listed dead were menu people, this sad dullard's kind of people. No lawyers died, no bankers, no financiers and speculators, no surveyors and stock-agents, no judges, journalists, restaurateurs, commodity dealers, generals, elected members of the Convention; in short, none of our kind of people. I ate well last winter. My fire never lacked wood, my table meat, my linen laundering, my horses exercise. Who shall be happy . . .? If . . .?

(*He's close but still it eludes him. He feels for it. The shot begins a slow tightening on his upturned face.*)

. . . Two summers back, in the rising I commanded from my room that overthrew King Louis the Last and changed our world into yours, better than three hundred gave up their lives that it might be so. Harness-makers, hairdressers, house-painters, carpenters, joiners, hatters, tailors, locksmiths, bootmakers, domestics, laundrymen, brickworkers, staymakers, waiters and scores upon scores of citizens 'below' these whom we in our wisdom had deemed too insignificant, that is too poor, to have the vote. Including two women from the market in Les Halles. All, once again, our Henry's kind of people. Who shall be happy . . .? Who?

(*The shot has closed right in.*)

For three whole years, we have been at war, with others and with ourselves. Who does the fighting, who does the dying? Robespierre? St Just? Danton?

(*He stops abruptly. Slowly turns.* HENRY's *back, stands the other side of the bars watching him, dealing with it all.*

Silence.)

HENRY: (*Finally*) It's the Serjeant's boy down from the Gate
  House. They wait my word. On the letter.

PRISONER: (*Quiet*) What did ye tell him?

HENRY: Ye didn't weep.

PRISONER: Weep?

HENRY: Ye said if ye told the story it'd mek ye weep. Ye didn't
  weep.
  (*Silence. They gaze at each other through the bars. Birdsong; a
  touch stronger, heading for sunrise.*
  Shot holds on the PRISONER's *face. Soundlessly, barely
  perceptibly, in real time, the eyes begin to fill, brim and spill.*)
  (*Blinking*) I told him to wait. Till I had answer.
  (*The tears grease the man's cheeks, nose, lips. More birdsong.*
  The room has gradually lightened a little; all but dawn.
  HENRY *heads once more for the doors. The man turns away, rests
  the back of his head on the bars, weeping still. He looks up at the
  lens, wordless.*)

PRISONER: (*Voice over; detached*) I touched him. I know it. He's
  touched.
  (HENRY *returns to the table. Broods. Flicks a look at the Cage.
  Begins to spread the greatcoat on the floor. The* PRISONER's *sunk
  to his haunches in the straw, his back against the side bars.*)

HENRY: (*Eventually; a touch annoyed*) It's sent. Go to sleep.
  (*The man sits on like a stone.*
  HENRY *lies on the greatcoat, stares at the Cage; finally shucks
  over on to his other side; lost.*
  *Wide shot of the room, the Cage, the still men. The dark
  continues to thin.*
  Birdsong; a blackbird.
  The PRISONER *reaches out a kerchief, begins wiping his face.*)

PRISONER: (*A mumble*) My last blackbird. Little fucker.
  (*Bring up fipple-flute and kettle-drum: 'Ça Ira', dreamlike.*
  *Cut to: close shot of his unblinking face staring up at the ceiling
  from the divan.*
  *His point of view through bars of the distressed paint and
  plasterwork ceiling.*

*His face again, the shot tighter. His eyes are closed. The lids
bobble on dreams.
Move through to sequence of mute dream images, random,
abrupt, rhythmed by the music; asynchronous sounds, discrete,
disconnected; his voice under, mumble, whisper, meditation,
coming and going.
Dawn. David's canvas* The Assassination of Marat *on an easel
in a clearing on a wooded river-bank. A blackbird perches on the
easel. The lapping of water.)*

PRISONER (*Voice over*): . . . Fêtes, pageants, plays, children's
stories, public buildings, costume, modes of address, the
names of seasons, years, months and days, songs, tunes,
dances, *moeurs*, custom, practice, ritual . . .
(*The prow of a flat-bottomed boat moving through water. Ropes
hang down from its side into the black of the river.*)
(*Voice over*) . . . We must create an Empire of Images. All
will be remade. We must colonize not just the minds . . .
(*The shot pans, following the underwater track of the ropes;
arrives at a second boat, to which they're attached. Bleed in the
roar of a vast crowd.*)
(*Voice over*) . . . but the very *lives* of the people.
(*Cut in: shot of a crisp blue sky. A bloodied arm appears, a
severed head, seen from behind, held aloft in the hand.*)
(*Voice over*) All will be remade . . .
(*Cut in: shot of thirty or so men and women, well-dressed,
digging a long trench under guard.*)
(*Voice over*) A new vocabulary for a new world order . . .
(*Return to: long shot of the flat-bottomed boat being poled out
into the estuary of the Loire. Sixty people or so, men, women,
children, bound hand and foot and roped to each other, stand on
its packed bottom.*)
(*Voice over*) . . . As, for example, 'vertical deportation',
Convention-Member Carrier's sublimely literary locution for
the happenings at Nantes . . .
(*Cut in: the trench, maybe two metres deep, the well-dressed
diggers gazing up towards the lip. Musket barrels poke down into
the shot: smoke; carnage.*)

30

(*Voice over*) . . . or Tallien's 'National Retrenchment' at
Lyons . . .

(*Return to: the boat again. Closer shot: priests; merchants; pious
peasants at silent prayer. Several uniformed soldiers move down
the boat, removing rings, watches, bracelets, necklets and items of
clothing and dropping them into the sacks they carry.*)

(*Voice over*) When I said. One year ago. When we were
young. 'Let *government* take terrible measures, so that the
people may not have to take them themselves' . . . Is this what
I had in mind?

(*Shot of the second, smaller boat, four soldiers rowing, six more
facing the first boat, guns in hands. They wear distinctive
headgear: a loosely wound plain linen cloth around the head; a
sort of turban à la Marat, as in David's canvas.*)

(*Voice over*) . . . Is it? The Marat Company? Obeying orders?

(*Close shot of turbanned head: a proud metal death's head badge
sits above the forehead,* 'Compagnie de Marat' *circling the metal
skull.*)

(*Voice over*) The Empire of Images. Virtue and Terror.
Hope, despair. Love, hate. Kind, vicious. Hot. Cold. This is
the inheritance, pale tiny faces in the gloom. Who shall be
happy if not . . . ? Not! Not!

(*The boats again, long, calm, peaceful, seen from distance,
approaching the middle of the estuary. The young day is already
beautiful.*

*The wooded bank again, the clearing, the canvas and easel, the
blackbird still in place. Slow creep in to Marat's angled,
turbanned head.*)

(*Voice over*) . . . And it was decreed that the sacred Empire
of Images should stretch to the world's edge and beyond.
And death would be no impediment. And lo! the great and
willing David, at a cost of not less than the annual earnings of
all the menu people of Nantes put together, defied Nature
for three whole days in high stinking summer so that the
blessed Martyr Marat's assassinated bodily remains might
tastefully, decently and enduringly preside in person over his
own funeral rites. Nature would be bettered. The body

would be emptied and stuffed, the knife-wounds
decorously diminished in size and stature for art's sake,
the distressing skin condition masked, the unusably
battered right arm that was to hold the telling steel pen
cut off and replaced with one in fuller working order from
the mortuary, the residual stench of natural decay
perfumed to sweetness, the unheroically lolling tongue slit
in four strategic sites to hold it steady . . . Never mind we
fight wars on four fronts, never mind the British blockade
shrivels supplies of food, never mind the country will soon
collapse into civil and atrocious war with itself . . . The
Empire of Images knows no nay and will be served . . .
(*The blackbird flaps abruptly off.*

The boats again; stopped now.

*In closer shot, we see polesmen and valuable-collectors leave
the large boat for the small one. Marat's men reach over the
side of the smaller boat, fish up the connecting ropes. As the
ropes tauten above the water line, we see they're tied to
temporary planking nailed to the larger boat and reaching
below the water line. Fipple-flute cuts; drum plays on.*)

(*Voice over*) . . . Did we imagine *this* would not be
remembered too? And. Built upon . . . ?

(*The oarsmen begin to pull their boat away. For a moment the
planks hold, turning the long boat into the current. Gradually,
one by one, they peel away, revealing the gaping holes they've
been plugging. Drum cuts.*

*The longboat sinks into the river. A great thrashing froth
develops around it, like a tuna harvest, as the* noyade
unfolds.)

(*Voice over*) Did Danton do this? Did any of us? For what?
To make the world a better place for our class of people?

(*Cut to: Cage.* PRISONER's *sleeping face, overhead shot, as
before. The lips mutter on.*)

. . . If not. Not. If not . . .

(*Fade to black.*

Fade up.

From black) Ye still there? Of course you are . . .

(*Long shot: Salle and Cage. Strong sunlight shafts in from above, reshaping the space.*
The PRISONER *stands at the table, all but naked, washing and sluicing his body with water from a large metal bowl.*)
Looking back's all that's left ye, *you* spent what was left of the future long since, you have nowhere else to look save back, do ye, poor sods . . . (*Looks at lens, smiles.*) For myself, and for my sins, I'm doomed to hope and chained to the present. (*He shakes his leg, rattling the chain at his ankle.*) The sixteenth day of Germinal in the Second Year of the Free Republic.
(HENRY *trudges up, a tray of food in his hands. The* PRISONER's *begun to dry himself. Sees* HENRY's *predicament, removes the bowl from the table, waits until* HENRY's *hands are free to take it from him.*
Fast cut to: room. Table. The PRISONER, *fully dressed, eats the food. White light cuts down across one shoulder, blacking out more than half his face and bleaching the remainder.*)
You are in my hands. Here, now. I feel you. We are the same flesh. Composed of the same atoms. Everything we have thought, everything we have tried or imagined, everything dreamt and whispered, designed, done . . . you will develop and perfect. Such a dish of worms we've served ye and ye'll eat 'em, every one. The free dance of capital, the human imperative. The sovereign people, the all-seeing all-saying State. Owner, worker. Nation and war, people and peace. The power of the machine, the machinery of power. Me, all. The impossible and the necessary dream. The road to freedom, mined every step of the way.
(*He sits back, wipes his mouth and hands with a linen cloth. Several bangs at the doors.* HENRY *appears in shot, headed down to answer. Sounds of his raised exchanges through the grille, as the man talks on.*)
(*Ignoring it*) And the question ye can no more answer than we can . . . the question you have perhaps begun to feel no longer *demands* an answer, since your recent unwitting witness to the meticulously staged death of history . . .

33

(*A brief commotion sets up at the doorway. Doors unlocked, angry words from* HENRY. *The doors relocked.* HENRY *stumps back up the room, another tray in his hands, a linen cloth spread over the contents.*
The PRISONER *watches, face taut now, reading the present.*
HENRY *lays the tray down on the table.*)

HENRY: This is not guard's work. Bastards. Ye done?
(*He takes the tray, lays it on the floor. The* PRISONER *stares at the new tray.*)
Your carriage's come. Ye leave at the half.
(*The* PRISONER *nods, stretches, turns to the Cage.*)
I've to cut your hair.

PRISONER: What?

HENRY: Cut your hair.

PRISONER: What for?

HENRY: Because I'm told to. I'm to lift the hair from your collar.
(*He removes the linen cloth: bowl, shears, combs, metal mirror. The* PRISONER *watches carefully.*)
Them's the orders. (*He gestures him to sit at the table.*)

PRISONER: (*Slow*) I understood the Man was still in trial, witnesses to be called, evidence to be heard . . .

HENRY: That was yesterday. You wanna sit, friend?
(*The* PRISONER *sits, face pale, still.* HENRY *combs out his back hair, sizing up the cut needed.*)
Trial's declared over. Jury's asked to proceed to judgment. Verdict's expected within the hour. S'what they say, how would I know . . . ?

PRISONER: If ye're cutting neck-hair, somebody knows, Henry . . .

HENRY: Happen.
(*He shears off a hand of hair, lays it on the table. The man stares at it. The shears hover for the next slice.*)

PRISONER: Poor sod.

HENRY: Maybe.
(*A second cut, another hand to the table. The* PRISONER *picks it up, examines it.*)

PRISONER: Hey.

34

HENRY: What?

PRISONER: Ye done this before?

HENRY: No.

PRISONER: I thought not. Don't send me out like a bloody page
boy, understood?

HENRY: This is Headsman's work.

PRISONER: Nevertheless.

HENRY: It'll grow.

PRISONER: Will it?

(*Silence.* HENRY *eventually resumes the cut.*)
He's dead then.

HENRY: Good as.

PRISONER: Poor sod.

HENRY: Why?

PRISONER: Why?

HENRY: Ye think he's innocent?

PRISONER: No one is innocent, friend . . .

HENRY: . . . Then he's guilty. Fuck him.

(*Silence.*)

PRISONER: Guilty of what?

HENRY: How should I know?

PRISONER: Guilty of what?

HENRY: Living fat off the people, how 'bout that . . . ?

PRISONER: That's most folk in britches, Henry.

HENRY: Ahunh.

(*Silence.* HENRY'*s all but finished. Holds up angled mirror.*)
Ye wanna see?

PRISONER: No.

(HENRY *begins to clear away and ferry trays down the room.*
Close shot of PRISONER, *hands on table, the fingers twitching as*
he broods.)
Is there word from your cousin?

HENRY: None. He'll be well abed by now.

PRISONER: And the letter . . . ?

HENRY: No word, no problem. It's done.

(*Town clock strikes the half. Silence. A brief look shared.*)

PRISONER: Ye're an honest man, Henry. I thank ye for your trust.

35

(HENRY *heads off with the second tray.*)

(*Flicking a glance at the lens*) So. The farce ends. Almost time
for last words . . . Clop across the Pont-au-Change, pass the
Quai de la Mègisserie, along the Rue de la Monnaie, down the
Rue Honoré to the Rue National, a wave for the terrace of the
Café du Montparnasse – Gabrielle, Louise – And . . . Eh *voilà!*
. . . Place de la Révolution. Where all this . . . history began.
Alpha and Omega. The first and the last. Full circle. I am
here. Last words then. What shall they be? Be sure to show
them my head, it's worth seeing . . . ? Let the Committee take
my head, the people already have my heart . . . ? (*Starts
chuckling.*) Now ye see me, now ye don't . . . ?

(*Banging at the doors again. He turns, peers at* HENRY *talking
through the grille.*)

(*Still dealing with last words*) . . . No, I should leave with a
question . . . (*He stands, puts his hands behind his back as if
tied, gazes out across the muted throng*) WHO SHALL BE
HAPPY . . . ? IF . . . ? WHO SHALL BE HAPPY, IF
NOT . . . ? IF *NOT* . . . ?

(HENRY *up the room sharpish, fiddling a length of rope from his
pocket.*)

HENRY: Your cart's stood by, you're to be readied, the Guards're
on their way . . .

(*He wraps the rope around the* PRISONER'*s wrists, still behind
his back, secures them, begins to detach the chain from the Cage
and convert it into leg-irons.*

The PRISONER *stands mute for some moments, looks down at the
cack-handed lad at his feet.*)

PRISONER: Cart, Henry?

HENRY: Cart, carriage . . .

(*In the silence, the sound of hooves, wheels on courtyard cobble
nearby.*)

PRISONER: So is there. A verdict through?

HENRY: (*Not looking*) Guilty. All charges.

(*He tugs at the second anklet. Stands. Eyes meet.*)

Ye right, are ye?

PRISONER: I'm searching for a question, Henry. Have to find it.

HENRY: It'll have to wait. (*Draws a leather hood from his pocket.*)
    Ye 'ave to leave as ye came . . .
    (*Silence.*)
PRISONER: (*Staring at it*) In our ends lie our beginnings . . . ?
HENRY: What?
PRISONER: Last words.
HENRY: Game's over. (*Prepares the hood.*) Orders.
    (*Silence. The* PRISONER *shuffles to the stool, sits, his back to the guard.* HENRY *quietly moves in behind him.*)
PRISONER: I see.
    (HENRY *bags the head, draws the cords, ties them.*)
HENRY: Ye breathin'?
    (*Close shot: hooded face. Only the lips are darkly visible, beyond the air-slit provided at the mouth.*
    He nods.
    HENRY *leaves the table area, gathering up his gear and belongings.*
    Close shot: PRISONER's *hooded face. Closes in to the vent, the barely seen mouth behind it.*)
PRISONER: (*A whisper*) I'm sixteen. I'm in Rheims. I'm standing in a long line of dignitaries clutching their cards of invitation outside the cathedral. My clothes are borrowed, the money for the journey stolen, but I will go through, I will see the young Louis anointed king, let him stop me who dares. The town police keep back the crowds. There are cheers for the queuing worthies, I find myself . . . waving acknowledgement. Just ahead, a clamour of beggars has wormed a way through the barricades and onto the steps of the West Door. Worthy coins appear on cue to soothe their noise, I fumble for a spare ten-sou piece, heart thumping I'll be found out . . .
    (*Long silence. Remote sounds of fists on doors down the room.*)
    One year ago. A day or so
    After.
    After.
    My Gabrielle. Birthing a dead
    daughter . . .

Died . . .
(*Silence.*)
And I had.
Detained in Belgium.
Back too late. Dug up her
corpse . . .
Detained in Belgium, did ye say . . . ?
Service to the Revolution the highest law
implied . . .? Pull the other
one, my friend, it plays
a tolerable version of
'Ça Ira'. In Belgium ye were
Looking out for yourself.
Doing deals, securing
Your loot, covering your tracks,
Saving France of course
And fucking
Everything in skirts
That moved.
(*Silence.*)
And knew. All
Along. She was like
To die.
With this one . . .
(*Silence. The lips move on, soundless.*
Cut to: profile shot of the hooded man deep enough to take in
HENRY *at the doors, admitting the two National Guard escorts.*
He stands them by in the doorway, trudges back towards the
table.)
No one is innocent.
Living's a guilty business . . .
HENRY: (*From distance*) Let's go.
PRISONER: (*Fast, urgent*) . . . A beggar reaches for my ten-sou
piece, his thick hand snaps around my wrist, I cannot shake
the bugger, the tocsin swells, I'll miss the King . . . The man
speaks: Ask him a question. Ask him a question. Come back
and tell me what he says. Ask him . . .

(HENRY's *arrived. Waits, frowning, in the growing silence.*)

HENRY: Let's go.

PRISONER: (*Simply*) Who shall be happy, if not everyone?

(*Silence.* HENRY *waves the guards in, taps the* PRISONER's *shoulder, helps him up.*)

Henry.

HENRY: What?

PRISONER: I'll say goodbye.

HENRY: Aye.

(*He passes him to the National Guardsmen. They lead him out. End titles begin.*

HENRY *scans the room. Gathers a few remaining odds and ends. Places them on or by the table for off. Picks up a lamp, lays it on a stool. Sits on the other stool, takes out watch, ring and purse of money, lays them out. The greatcoat joins them. He takes out his pipe. Can't find his flint. Reaches for his musket. Removes the furled letter from the barrel. Tapers it to the lamp. Lights his pipe.*

Fipple-flute and drum: 'Ça Ira'.

Long shot: Salle, Cage. Flute out; drum on alone.

HENRY *gathers his gear, trudges off.*

As the doors bang to behind him, the safety-curtain guillotine slices down.)

THATCHER'S CHILDREN

Thatcher's Children was first performed at the Old Vic, Bristol, on 19 May 1993. The cast was as follows:

MONA PATTERSON	Marva Alexander
TOM CLARE	Ian Driver
GURVINDER SINGH KUTHANI	Kulvinder Ghir
HESTER PATTERSON	Heather Imani
DAISY JAY	Miranda Pleasence
SANDRA COPE	Cassie Stuart
WAYNE RICHARDS	Giles Thomas
MUSICIANS	James Woodrow, Howard Gay

Director	Andrew Hay
Designer	Mick Bearwish
Lighting	Tim Streader
Music composition and direction	John O'Hara

ACT ONE

*Changing room, Leighley Juniors, lit from corridor. Evening. Buzz
and clack of parents arriving in adjacent Assembly Hall; sounds of
pop medley of Christmas carols on bad relay.*

GURVINDER *arrives, clicks on the lights, moves gravely into the
room. He's ten; two years in Britain, in Yorkshire one term.*

*He wears a floor-length overcoat, a makeshift wool turban, a
stove-pipe hat atop it; carries a long brush-stale and a Safeways
plastic bag. He stands facing out, lips quivering, close to tears.
Sits. Removes hat and turban, reveals a beautifully wrought head
of Sikh braids. Takes out a draw-string marble-bag from his
pocket, fishes out a pair of scissors, slowly begins to cut the braids.
On the final snip, the lights suddenly dim, flutter, surge back, as the
grid heads for overload. The boy looks fearfully up, sensing
judgement.*

*Voices from corridor. Laughter. Teachers' shushes. The lights
bobble again, appear to steady; abruptly cut.*

*Hubbub from hall, corridors. The Headmistress's voice rises above
the din to announce contingency plans involving storm lamps,
should the power cut persist. Some ironic parent applause.*

*Class teacher's voice in corridor, detailing 4H to take lamps with
them. Children appear, lamps in hand, nattering and giggling as
they go, move in to occupy the now empty room.*

CLASS TEACHER: (*Off; after them*) Has anybody seen Sandra?
  Hester . . .
  (*They fall silent, attentive, as if she were in the room.*)
HESTER: (*Black; eleven; dressed as Wise Man*) No, Miss. Don't
  think she's come yet, Miss.
TEACHER: (*Off*) Oh my God, that's all we need . . . What is
  she . . . ?
HESTER: First Virgin Mary, Miss.
MONA: (*Her sister, ten; a heavily pillow-pregnant black Virgin
  Mary*) Second.
HESTER: First, you're second . . .

43

TEACHER: All right, all right. Mona, you can do both, all right?

MONA: I can't, I don't know t'words, Miss . . .

HESTER: I know them, Miss, I'll teach her them . . .

(*Mona pulls a face.*)

TEACHER: Thank you, Hester. (*To another group across the way; seamlessly.*) Shepherds! Stop talking! Yes that does mean you, Darren Claypole! (*To them again.*) Right, go over your lines with each other and be ready when you're called.

DAISY: (*Angel Gabriel as the Good Fairy*) Miss, Gurvinder's not here either, Miss . . .

TEACHER: (*Off*) Jesus Ch . . . Wouldn't you just know it . . . Has anyone seen him?

WAYNE: (*Minimal Innkeeper; a large ten, from Pontypridd; one term up from Wales*) I seen him, Miss.

TEACHER: (*Off*) When was that, Wayne?

WAYNE: (*Giggling*) This mornin', Miss.

(*Laughter, which they try to sit on.*)

TEACHER: (*Off; to corridor; loud*) Have any of you children seen Gurvinder Kurthani . . . ?

GURVINDER: (*Hidden in room; tiny voice*) Here, Miss . . .

TEACHER: (*Off*) Gurvinder, are you there . . . ?

GURVINDER: (*Crawling out*) Yes, Miss.

(*The children hold up their lamps to light his passage*)

TEACHER: (*Off*) You're going to have to speak up, Gurvinder, you're in Yorkshire now, no one hears you in Yorkshire unless you shout . . . Good, go over your lines, please, and stay put . . . (*Seamless segue, to the clatter of feet in corridor*) *Walk*, Roman Soldiers . . . How many more times . . .

(*She's gone. The group stare at the young re-turbanned Sikh, who lies face down on the floor sobbing.*)

MONA: What's the matter with him? What's a matter with ye, Girlie?

WAYNE: Er, he's skrikin', Girlie's skrikin', mardy bugger . . .

DAISY: Oh *do* shut up, Wayne . . .

MONA: He's always sayin' right stupid things, 'im . . .

(DAISY *and* MONA *move in to comfort the* SIKH. TOM's *already*

there, in Joseph costume, a wire coat-hanger in his hand which
he's been struggling to fit around his tea-towel kuffiah since
arriving.)

TOM: (*Squatting; ten; pale, shy, well-spoken*) Come on, Girlie, it's
all right, you don't need to cry . . .

DAISY (*Elbowing* TOM) . . . It's all right, I'll look after him . . .

MONA: (*Close in*) Come on, Girlie, we've gotta do it in a minute
. . . you're gonna ruin everythin'.

DAISY: Poor Gurvinder.

TOM: He might be sick.

WAYNE: (*Fiddling with his 'Pontypridd Baths' towel in his*
waistband) Er, don't touch 'im, ye'll catch the lurgi . . .
(*The girls tell him to shut up.* DAISY *whacks at him with her*
wand. He backs off, well pleased. The girls close in, concern
rising. Even HESTER, *who's been running her lines, draws in to*
look.)

TOM: Shall I tell Miss?

DAISY: Gurvinder. What's happened? Are you poorly? Mm?
What's up?
(*The boy rolls suddenly over onto his back, laughter pouring from*
him. The girls recover, begin punching and joshing him.)
(SANDRA *has appeared unseen from the Hall side. Stands in the*
darkness watching the mêlée; she's ten, sad-faced, a perfect white
Virgin Mary.)

MONA: (*As the weird laughter drains away*) . . . Tell us
wharrappened, will ye, ye're goin' ruin everythin' . . .

GURVINDER: (*Grave, sullen*) I cut me hair.

HESTER: You didn't.

GURVINDER: I did . . .

DAISY: What did your dad say?

GURVINDER: He 'an't seen it.

MONA: Ye kiddin' again, aren't ye?

GURVINDER: Not.

DAISY: (*Arms around him*) Oh Gurvinder.

WAYNE: Er, Daisy Jay's snoggin' Girlie . . .

MONA: 'E's kiddin' us.

TOM: Are you?

(*The boy shakes his head.*)

DAISY: Are you?

(*He sits up. Removes his turban. They stare at the shorn head.*
TOM's *hand wavers towards it, hovers, trapped between want and
don't.* WAYNE *moves in to have a look.*)

(*Feeling the head; fearless*) Oh, it's really soft.

WAYNE: (*Smirky*) Like 'is 'ead.

(MONA *feels it.*)

DAISY: (*To* TOM) Feel it.

MONA: Are you gonna tell us why ye cut it, Girlie?

HESTER: (*To* MONA) Come on, I've got to teach you Sandra's lines . . .

MONA: You're not my mother, ye know . . .

HESTER: You heard what Miss said . . .

MONA: (*Defiant*) Come on, Girlie, tell us why you cut it.

GURVINDER: (*Standing*) So's they wunt call us Girlie.

(*Silence.*

*The lights plunge up abruptly, bobble, hold, to ironic cheers and
clapping from the audience in the Hall; cut again, to groans off.*
the HEADMISTRESS's *voice rears again: they'll begin at seven,
come what may. Applause.*)

In the brief illumination, the group becomes aware of SANDRA *at
the back of the room. Her face has creased and grown wet with
anguish.*)

WAYNE: Oh God, not another skriker.

(SANDRA *blubs on, immersed in the pain of things.*)

DAISY: What is it? Where've you been? What's happened?

SANDRA: Miss told Mona to learn my words . . .

WAYNE: 'Cos you weren't 'ere, stupid.

SANDRA: I was . . .

DAISY: Poor Sandra.

WAYNE: Boo hoo.

SANDRA: . . . I was lookin' t'see if me mam'd come . . .

DAISY: Has she?

SANDRA: (*Worse*) No . . .

DAISY: Listen, don't cry, it'll ruin your face . . .

HESTER: (*Decisive*) What's the problem? She's here now, she can
do her part . . .

46

SANDRA: She doesn't like me, Miss Hutchison . . .

WAYNE: Nobody bloody likes you, girl . . . S'cos you stink, see, boohoohoo . . .

(SANDRA's wails grow worse, WAYNE sniggers, pleased with himself. GURVINDER brings him a wholly unlooked-for clout over the head with his broom-stale. WAYNE yelps, doubles over, head in hands.)

Aah aah aah, you stupid bugger, what d'you do that for . . . ? *(GURVINDER puts a finger to his lips: say no more.)* . . . I'll bloody get you for that, you little sod . . . You're bloody barmy, d'you know that?

(He makes an unconvincing show of retaliating.)

GURVINDER: *(Stick raised again)* I'm a king, me.

HESTER: Gurvinder. Put that down and get ready. Come on, I'll help you . . .

GURVINDER: All friends, all friends.

(He returns to sit meekly between HESTER's legs to have his turban tied. DAISY and MONA begin repairing SANDRA's face. WAYNE worries at the bump on his head, checking for blood. TOM can't get the wire coat-hanger to fit on his head. Bits and bobs of lines get rehearsed throughout.)

TOM: Can someone help me with this, please?

MONA: Come 'ere.

(He sits by her, hands her the hanger, she sizes up the job. GURVINDER fiddles a thermos from his plastic bag.)

HESTER: *(Finishing touches)* What you brought that for?

GURVINDER: Miss told me to.

HESTER: What for?

GURVINDER: 'S for me myrrh.

HESTER: Do you know your words?

GURVINDER: Is it a star? Is it a sign? I must follow it as far as Leeds, me.

HESTER: As far as it leads me.

GURVINDER: Yes.

TOM: What's your dad going to say when he sees your hair?

GURVINDER: Nothing.

SANDRA: Have you cut your hair?

GURVINDER: No.

SANDRA: Y'ave.

GURVINDER: Haven't.

MONA: He'll kill ye, won't 'e?

GURVINDER: He won't.

MONA: You'll get the belt.

GURVINDER: I won't.

TOM: I bet he won't take you to Gotscam Chairs this weekend.

GURVINDER: He will.

DAISY: Is he coming tonight?

GURVINDER: I don't know.

DAISY: He is, isn't he?

GURVINDER: He might be.

SANDRA: Have ye kept it?

(THE SIKH *shows them the marble-bag.*)

GURVINDER: 'S in there.

MONA: Ye can sell it, ye know. I saw it on t'tele.

WAYNE: Gerroff.

MONA: I did.

WAYNE: Who'd wanna buy that?

HESTER: (*Setting stove-pipe hat on* GURVINDER'*s head*) Where's your glass, Wayne?

WAYNE: 'S on the stage where I left it.

HESTER: What about the pretend cigarette Miss gave you . . . ?

WAYNE: Oh shit, I knew there was something . . .

(*He searches his roll-bag, muttering.*)

TOM: Shall I help you look for it?

MONA: (*Still at work on the hanger*) Sit still, you.

WAYNE: Bloody 'ell, 'ow'll they know I'm an innkeeper if I don't 'ave a fag . . . ?

(DAISY *whispers something in* MONA'*s ear.* MONA *giggles.*)

SANDRA: My dad always has a fag.

WAYNE: Aw, 'e bloody would, wouldn'e . . . ?

SANDRA: Behind his ear. 'Cos he's an innkeeper.

WAYNE: (*Searching pockets*) That's not an inn, that's a pub . . .

DAISY: (*Fumbling a ten-pack of Craven A from her knickers*) You can borrow one of these if you like.

48

WAYNE: (*Crossing*) 'S'ave a look. (*She opens the packet. He takes one gingerly.*) Where'd you get 'em?

DAISY: My mum left them on the Welsh dresser.
(WAYNE *gains confidence. Pretends to smoke it. Tries tucking it behind his ear.*)

MONA: It dunt look right, that.

WAYNE: Course it does.

DAISY: Mona's right, it's the cork tip, it's wrong.

WAYNE: How d'ye mean?

DAISY: They didn't have cork tips in those days.

TOM: (*Quiet*) They didn't actually have cigarettes.
(*Silence. They all stare at him. He colours up.*)

DAISY: Here. Try one of her roll-ups. She always does a couple before she goes out. See. No tip.
(WAYNE *takes the roll-up; frowns at it.* DAISY *holds a lighter out, clicks on the flame.*)

WAYNE: 'S that for?

DAISY: You have to smoke it a bit, then dimp it and put it behind your ear, like Sandra's dad.

WAYNE: 'E 'as a *pub* . . .

MONA: Er, look at 'im, mardy bugger . . .

WAYNE: I aren't mard . . .

MONA: 'Ere y'are, give it 'ere, I'll smoke it . . .

HESTER: Don't you dare . . .

WAYNE: No, you won't . . .
(*He ducks down for the light. Comes up puffing. Splutters a bit. Applause, laughter from the group.* HESTER *turns away, disgusted.*)

MONA: 'Ey, ye look right good wi' that, Wayne.

WAYNE: Course I do.
(*He smokes on, posing and strutting.*)

MONA: (*Leaning back, clutching her pillow*) Aagh, aagh . . .

TOM: What's wrong?

MONA: I'm pregnant. I think me waters're bursting . . . Feel it.
(TOM *very delicately lays a hand on her huge middle.* MONA *slaps it.*)
Not too hard . . .

SANDRA: (*To* WAYNE) Save some for behind your ear. (*Finger and thumb.*) About that much . . .
(*The piano strikes up by the stage, a buzz and applause as the first and second years troop out to sing the Shepherds' song.*
The kids tingle into readiness, little hums of nerves from the girls, exaggerated gesturing from the lads.)

CLASS TEACHER: (*Hall side now; low; distinct*) . . . Hester, Gurvinder, Daisy, stand by please, you're on when the song ends, all right, just as we did in rehearsal, Daisy first . . .

HESTER/DAISY/GURVINDER: Yes, Miss.

GURVINDER: Miss?

CLASS TEACHER: (*Off*) What is it, Gurvinder?

GURVINDER: (*Worried sick*) Has me dad come, Miss . . . ?

CLASS TEACHER: (*Off*) Gurvinder, how would I know . . . ?

GURVINDER: He wears a turban, Miss . . .

WAYNE: (*Another puff*) And a skirt.

CLASS TEACHER: (*Off*) Thank you for sharing that with us, Wayne. Now *shut* up, the lot of you, and stand by . . .
(WAYNE *giggles, out of control. Others join in;* HESTER *and* DAISY *try to quiet them. The Shepherds' song draws to a ragged close. Vast parent applause. Third Year Roman Soldiers thud on and disperse the Shepherds with shouts and blows.*
DAISY *walks out, calm and straight, her wand aloft. We follow her.*)

DAISY: Beebeebeebee. I am the Angel Gabriel . . .
(*She stops suddenly.* GURVINDER *has followed her.* HESTER *whispers him back, off; too late.*)

GURVINDER: Is it a star? Is it a sign?
(*They stare at each other.* GURVINDER *realizes something's wrong, makes as if to leave.*)

DAISY: (*To him*) I am the Angel Gabriel. Pray tell me who you might be?
(*Silence. The boy has no lines.* HESTER *appears suddenly.*)

HESTER: We are two Wise Persons following that bright star in the East.
(*Silence.*)

GURVINDER: (*Suddenly*) I am a king, me.
(*They look at him.*)

50

HESTER: We bring gifts, gold, frankincense and myrrh . . .
 (GURVINDER *holds up his thermos flask*) . . . for the child about
 to be born.
 (GURVINDER *turns to leave.* HESTER *grabs his arm to stop him.*
 The top hat falls from his head. As he stoops to collect it the turban
 follows.
 GURVINDER *freezes, on the edge of tears.* HESTER *stoops, tries to*
 set the hat on his head.)
GURVINDER: I must follow it as far as Leeds, me . . .
DAISY: Good. Beebeebeebeebee.
 (*She disappears.* HESTER *leads* GURVINDER *off.*)
GURVINDER: (*Distraught mutters*) . . . I lost me turban, me dad saw
 me hair, he won't tek me to God's Armchair now . . .
 (TOM *appears, drawing a stool behind him on a piece of rope.*
 MONA *trots after him, straddles the stool with difficulty, follows*
 him at a crouch around the stage.)
MONA: Joseph, Joseph, we must find a place to stay, I'm almost
 ready to have the baby . . .
TOM: I'll try this inn, shall I?
MONA: Yes, yes, try that inn.
 (TOM *knocks. Steps back. They wait.* MONA *gestures him to knock*
 again. TOM *steps forward, knuckles ready.*)
WAYNE: (*Off*) Hello? Who is it?
TOM: Mary and Joseph.
 (*Long silence.* WAYNE *appears, glass in hand, roll-up dimped and*
 wedged behind ear.)
WAYNE: What do you want?
MONA: We have travelled a long way and I'm tired and I'm
 pregnant. Do you have a room?
 (*Long pause.* WAYNE *gazes upward, as if in another dimension.*)
WAYNE: Yes.
 (*Silence.* MONA *and* TOM *look at each other, aghast.* WAYNE
 smiles fondly at them, well pleased.)
TOM: (*Finally*) Miss!
 (*The stage lights suddenly come on, flooding them with dawn light.*
 They freeze.
 HESTER, GURVINDER, SANDRA *and* DAISY *appear from the*

wings, propelled by the desperate CLASS TEACHER, *join the others at the front of the stage.*
    Piano. Guitar. They sing.)
ALL: Hello, Mr Sunnyman,
        Lift your sleepy head,
        All night you've kept us waiting
        While you've been in your bed.

        Come along, Mr Sunnyman,
        Spread your lovely light,
        Fill the world with goodness
        And love and peace, all right?
    (*Slow fade to black.*)

Image of green roller-blackboard. On it, chalked up in teacher's hand:
   'FOR ME, THE HEART OF POLITICS IS NOT POLITICAL THEORY,
IT IS PEOPLE AND HOW THEY WANT TO LIVE THEIR LIVES.'
Copy out two hundred times and hand in to the Headmaster's
Office not earlier than 5 pm.
    The image holds, dies.
    Bring up: SANDRA, *in spot, facing out, copying out in exercise book, voicing each slow word she writes. She lifts her head to check the board (out front now); she carries an ugly bruise on her left cheek.*
    Bring up: class room, comprehensive school; late afternoon, late spring. WAYNE, MONA *and* SANDRA *spread around the room, copy out their lines. They're Fifth Year, C stream.*
SANDRA: . . . people and how they want to live their lives full stop
    (*checks board*) for me comma . . .
GURVINDER: (*In at speed from corridor*) . . . I don't believe it. I just
    seen Tom an' DJ. Who busted ye . . . ?
    (*They shush him, gesture the stock-room out front.*)
WAYNE: (*Sotto*) Ratface.
GURVINDER: Fuck this, I'm gonna 'ave a word . . .
SANDRA: Don't, you'll mek things worse . . .
GURVINDER: (*At stock-room door; downstage; the teacher invisible
    and unheard throughout*) 'Scuse me, sir, could I 'ave a
    word . . . ? Well, it's just couldn't ye let 'em go, sir? We're
    goin' campin' this weekend up the Dales an' we got train

tickets 'n' stuff, ye know . . . (*Listens to Ratface.*) No, I'm not sayin' that, sir, ye could keep 'em in next Monday, it's just it's Sandra's birthday an' it's all arranged . . . (*Listens again.*) Aw, go on, sir . . . Why not? Ye gonna ruin everythin' . . . Ye could. Course ye could. Why not? Give us one good reason . . . Y'aven't got one, that's why . . . (*low.*) Oh fuck off, ye little shit . . . (*Moves back into room. Returns to answer him.*) I said fuck off, ye little shit!

(*He heads back towards his desk, searches angrily for his gear.*)

MONA: (*Chewing gum*) Ey, cool it, Girlie, ye know Ratface . . .

(*Eyes swivel to the stock-room door.*)

GURVINDER: (*Still searching*) Sod him.

(*Looks up as Ratface speaks.*)

I'm looking for me gear. No, I won't, it's me dad's, I left it here . . . (*Listens, eyes hardening*) Ye put it *where*, what ye put it there for? I'm askin' you a question . . . *Junk?* Ye callin' it junk, ye . . . racist pig? I'll bloody junk you, if that gear's damaged you're in trouble, mate. Serious.

(*He's heading out. Ratface says something.*)

. . . I'm out of 'ere in four weeks, chum, you can't do nothin' . . . I'll be back . . . Serious.

(*Silence. The three watch; return as one to their chore as the teacher turns to look at them.*)

ALL: (*Responding as he follows after* GURVINDER) Yes, sir.

(*He's gone.* WAYNE's *on his feet, follows to the corridor door, chunner and double V-signs, pissed off.* MONA *lights up, hands it to* SANDRA, *who puffs at it nervously, worried she'll be caught.*)

MONA: We could just go.

WAYNE: No way. They'll just sling us out, look what they did to Darren Thingie . . .

MONA: Let 'em. I don't mind. What ye think?

SANDRA: No. I couldn't. Me dad'd kill us . . .

MONA: He'd kill ye if 'e knew you were goin' campin' up Malham, too, what's the diff . . . ?

SANDRA: 'S different, that's all.

(WAYNE *takes the cigarette from her, draws deep.*)

WAYNE: I gotta get my exams, see. But I tell you what: if I ever

get into uniform, I'll have that little fucker for this, see if I don't . . .
(HESTER *appears, books in hand, not privy to the planned weekend.*)

MONA: What do you want?

HESTER: Are you still spending the weekend at Carmen Johnson's?
(WAYNE *and* SANDRA *give* MONA *a look.*)

MONA: Yeah, why?

HESTER: No reason. (*Takes in blackboard.*) Who busted you?

WAYNE: Bloody Ratcliffe.

HESTER: What for?

WAYNE: Nowt.

HESTER: (*To* MONA *again*) So Mum'll be able to call you there if she needs to, will she?

MONA: Aye, if she can find a phone that works in Harehills . . .

HESTER: If she needs to, she'll find one.

MONA: What's it to you, anyway?

HESTER: Not much. Only I just saw Carmen getting on the Field Trip bus to the Lakes.

MONA: So?

HESTER: So? So what're you playing at?

MONA: Mind your own bloody business, will ye . . .

HESTER: You'd better tell me, our Mona . . .

MONA: Mind your own business, will ye, I can look after meself, thank you, what are you, bloody KGB . . . ?
(DAISY *arrives,* TOM *in her wake, both keenly got out for camping. Each carries a huge backpack, bedrolls, tentrolls, pans, tin mugs hanging neatly down from them.*)

DAISY: (*Glancing at stock-room, low-voiced*) . . . Hopeless, I rang the station, it's the last train . . .

WAYNE: Fuck.

DAISY: So. Another great idea bites the dust . . .

MONA: 'S all right, he's not there, Girlie threw a moody, he's legged it after 'im . . .

HESTER: Last train to where?

TOM: Craven. We were meant to be camping out at Gotscam Chairs . . .

54

DAISY: Sandra's birthday. Bugger. (*She puts her hand on* SANDRA*'s shoulder*.) Never mind, you can stay at my Mum's, we'll have a party . . .

SANDRA: Doesn't matter. Honest.

DAISY: (*The bruise*) How'd you get that?

SANDRA: 'S nothing. (*Beat*) I ran into a lamp-post comin' t'school . . .

(DAISY *gives* TOM *a look.* HESTER *has fixed a withering glare on* MONA. MONA *gets up, lights another cigarette, crosses to the doorway, stares out down the corridor.*)

TOM: (*From nowhere*) We could go. (DAISY *turns, looks at him.*) There's time . . .

DAISY: Tom. There are times you are just . . . so selfish. It's Sandra's birthday present, she's the whole point of it . . .

TOM: Yes, I know . . .

DAISY: Well, then.

MONA: Right on.

WAYNE: Hellfire, listen 'em. That's women all over for you, one down the toilet, all down the toilet. I understand, Thomas boy. All you're seeing's a golden opportunity to get your little end away goin' up in smoke, right boyo?

(TOM *blushes and laughs, stranded between the two.* SANDRA *laughs too.*)

SANDRA: You're a dirty beggar, Wayne Richards.

WAYNE: (*Leering*) Aren't I just.

(*He makes for her, pretending to undo his fly as he goes.* SANDRA *purrs behind her pretend shrieks.*)

MONA: Ratface!

(*Rapid adjustments in the room.*)

'S OK. He's turned into t'Staff Room.

WAYNE: I wish 'e'd turn into a corpse. Little prick.

DAISY: You wouldn't have a word with him, would you, Hes? If he lets 'em go now, we could still make it . . . Come on, you know he fancies you . . .

HESTER: Do me a favour.

MONA: She won't help.

TOM: 'S worth a try, Hes.

HESTER: What are you supposed to have done?

WAYNE: Nowt. I told you.

SANDRA: It was, it was nowt, he was tekin' us for social studies an'
he was dronin' on an' on about what a good thing the election
was for this country, we're gonna see some changes, unions and
workers and us lot are in for a rude awakenin', on an' on like, oh
yeah an' like last winter they couldn't bury the dead an' that an'
then Wayne said . . . (*giggling*) What did ye say . . . ? Go on . . .

WAYNE: Nowt. I just told 'im we couldn't get anyone to bury my
grandad an' he said, 'cos o' the strike, right? An' I said, no,
'cos 'e wasn't dead . . .
(SANDRA *and* MONA *start laughing.* DAISY *joins in.* TOM *follows.*
Hester waits.)

HESTER: And what about you?

SANDRA: I laughed.

MONA: Me too.

HESTER: And Gurvinder?

WAYNE: Girlie was over doin' someat wi' their lot in Multicultural
Studies . . .

DAISY: Yeah, he was brill . . .

TOM: Brought his dad's gear – the five Ks – told us what it all
meant, amazing . . .

DAISY: Come on, Hes.

HESTER: (*Leaving*) I'll see what I can do. But whatever happens,
she's not going, not unless she asks our mum first . . .

MONA: (*After her*) . . . Ye make me sick, you . . .

HESTER: Mutual.
(*She's gone.* DAISY *holds up crossed fingers.* SANDRA *smiles*
palely. MONA *dimps her fag, still on watch.*)

WAYNE: (*Examining* TOM) Nice gear.

TOM: It's my brother's.

WAYNE: Bet that cost a packet.

TOM: I don't know.

MONA: Right, she's collared him . . .
(*They listen.* MONA *peeps out occasionally, as* HESTER *tackles*
Ratcliffe. Her voice gets closer, as she trails him up the corridor.
MONA *legs it back to her desk as he returns.*)

DAISY: (*To his question*) . . . We're just waiting for our friends, sir. (*She pulls a face, reluctantly heads for the corridor, pushing* TOM *ahead of her, to wait outside.*)

HESTER: (*From doorway*) . . . Excuse me, sir, I don't think you have the right to do this, they're going to lose a lot of money on rail tickets and things . . . (*She cuts as he shouts at her.*) Sir, threats are no substitute for argument . . . (*He says something else.*) Fine, I'll see if the Headmaster'll deal with it . . . (*She walks off, calm and tough.* DAISY *and* TOM *push out into the corridor.*)

WAYNE/MONA/SANDRA: (*Replying*) Yes, sir. (*They watch him into his lair. Relax.* WAYNE *gives him the double V-sign.*)

SANDRA: I really like your sister.

MONA: Ye can 'ave 'er. (*Suppressed giggles, which cut as the teacher reappears in the stock-room doorway.*)

MONA: (*Replying, eyes down*) Yes, sir. (*They work under his gaze for some moments.*)

WAYNE: Sir, who wrote this, was it Mrs Thatcher, sir . . . ? (*A roaring rumpus down the corridor, heading their way.*

TOM: (*From corridor*) Hey up, Girlie, what're you . . . ? (*Heads swivel.* GURVINDER *appears at speed through the door, dressed in his dad's gear [turban, keche, kara], a solid steel kirpan in his hands. Dives straight for Ratcliffe, scimitar outstretched. Stops a foot or two from his face, eyes burning.*)

GURVINDER: (*In Punjabi*) 'One for all and all for one. Praise the Lord.' (*He motions him with the sword to leave the room. Follows him with his eyes to the door.*) (*After him, responding*) Yeah, sure. Go an' get the cavalry, you don't scare me, Ratface . . .

WAYNE: Wow, fuckin' Bruce Lee . . . (*Laughter released; anxiety too; it was heavy, for a while.* GURVINDER *laughs, a kid again.*)

DAISY: That was brill, Girlie, but maybe you should scarper . . .

MONA: Right. He's a mean bugger, is Ratface . . .

TOM: Yeah.

GURVINDER: (*Fast*) No. No no no. (*Sword outstretched again.*) All friends, all friends, hands please. (*He gestures them to place their palms on the blade. Frowns, giggles.*) We will do it. We will do it.

TOM: Do what, Girlie?

GURVINDER: Hands, please. I show you . . .

WAYNE: (*Offering hand*) Don't cut the bugger off, will you . . . (*Other hands follow, cover the blade. Some laughter, joshing, dying away.* HESTER *returns, watches from the doorway.*)

GURVINDER: (*In Punjabi, then translates*) All for one, one for all, praise the Lord. (*In Punjabi again, then translates.*) We swear by this holy weapon to make our way together one day, some time, to the place called God's Armchair.

DAISY: Gotscam Chairs.

GURVINDER: Yes. All swear.
(*They swear, somewhere between embarrassment and fascination.*)

HESTER: On your bike, Girlie, Ratcliffe's called the pigs . . .

GURVINDER: No. You too. Hand, please . . .

SANDRA: You've gotta split, Girlie . . .

GURVINDER: Hand. Please.

HESTER: Me? Why?

GURVINDER: Because I love you.

HESTER: What?

MONA: Do it. He's gonna get busted . . .
(*He holds out the sword. She moves in.*)

HESTER: I swear.

GURVINDER: All right. Fuck 'em.
(*Fast black.*)

Bring up:

THATCHER'S VOICE: (*Tape; echoic*) Where there is discord, may we bring harmony.
    Where there is error, may we bring truth.
    Where there is doubt, may we bring faith.
    Where there is despair, may we bring hope.

Bring up: image of Thatcher. It stays for some time, presiding over what follows. MONA, *Tesco check-out, the work unrelenting.*

MONA: (*Out; speaking around the process*) What d'ye think? Great, eh? YOP scheme. Youth Opportunity. I should be so lucky. Still, it's better than waxin' chickens for Plumleys Plumptious. Not a lot, mind . . . (*To customer*) D'you want a bag for them? (*Hands her one. Moves on.*) £32.50 a week for 48 hours. Good, eh? Never mind, I'm off out tonight. Clubbin'. See what's 'appening'. (*Checks her queue*) God, look at 'em. They've all been lookin' for the '500 items and over' till and fetched up wi' me. Ah well. Only one thing for it. (*Takes out a hairpin, carefully jams it in her till. Several tings, the till goes down. Presses buzzer. Calls.*) Supervisor, please! Till 15.

(*She crosses her legs, swivels in her seat, rubs an emery board across her nails, flashes us a smile.*

Her light cuts. Sound of doorknocker.

Bring up: GURVINDER, *briefcase, jacket, spruced up.*)

GURVINDER: (*As door opens*) Good morning, madam, I wonder if I can interest you in my company's revolutionary range of herbal health products . . .? (*The door closes in his face. He turns, gazes out; perfect Tommy Cooper:*) Just like that. (*Light out.*

Bring up: SANDRA, *in long blonde wig, bedroom above rowdy pub. She's deep in thought, dressing up in her mother's clothes before a mirror. Mumbles to herself as she becomes a notional glamorous other.*)

SANDRA: That's not right. She needs to be more . . . (*She works on.*) That's more like it. If ye've gorrit, flaunt it.

(*Hears sound on landing, swivels, freezes.*)

DAD'S VOICE: You asleep, girl?

SANDRA: (*Sleepy.*) Yes, dad.

(*All clear. She clips on bits of Ratners' here and there, poses this way, that. Hunts for something. Comes up with a red garter, puts it on, begins reworking cheekbones, eyes. Pouts, sticks her bum out in the tight dress: Marilyn. Fits a cigarette butt into a long plastic holder, checks for danger below, lights it; soignée.*

What d'ye think, Mum?

(She stares at herself for a long time in silence. Air slowly leaves her; form and face crumple. She removes the wig, revealing her spiked mouse beneath. Picks up the lipstick again. Draws a raw vertical slash down her face: forehead, nose, mouth, chin. Stares on. The light shrinks to the face.
Bring up: DAISY, *night, self-chained by the wrist to flower-decked MOD wire fence, in* People's Right to Work *campaign T-shirt, jeans and Docs, a* No to Cruise *placard propped beside her. Women call each other along the perimeter, locating, encouraging, supporting. Sirens, car, men's voices, MOD police boots on gravel. A searchlight up, scanning fence. It picks up* DAISY. *She's scared, firm.)*

DAISY: *(Calling)* Mum. You OK? *(Indistinct reply.)* Yeah, sure, I'm fine.

(Men's voices, raised. Sounds of boots on the trot. The lights shrink down to her face. Sound of doorknocker. Cut light. Bring up:)

GURVINDER: Good morning, madam, I'm doing a survey on behalf of the local council regarding house contents insurance . . . *(Door closes, he swivels into follow-spot to face out, mike in hand, to laughter from working men's club audience.)* . . . Ye've gorra laugh, 'aven't ye . . . Anyone 'ere got a job? *(Someone puts his hand up.)* Mine's a pint. I'm down the dole office, right, the Black Hole, bottom of Eastgate, run by really lovely people. I reach the counter, this clerk says, Oh Christ not another bloody nigger, I says, I beg your pardon!, He leans forward, takes another look, he says I'm sorry . . . Paki, I said, I should think so too. Guy next to me's on crutches, one leg, he's complainin' he's had his disability allowance cut, the clerk says he can't help, there's too much dependency, he says, people've gotta learn to stand on their own two feet . . . I thought, that's a good idea, I'll go out and sell what I don't need . . . So I sold all me pockets . . . Anyroad, I'm walkin' 'ome, mindin' me own business . . .

(The follow-spot dies. Flames begin to burn out the image of Thatcher.

Bring up: sounds of inner city riots: burning buildings, voices at full pitch, the pop and smash of petrol bombs.
Something lands at GURVINDER's *feet, he stoops to pick it up: it's a milk bottle, half-filled with petrol, the top stuffed with a charred rag. A sharp siren close by, cars screech in, doors slam, hurled voices, boots at the double.* GURVINDER *backs away, searches for escape: nowhere to run.*
Fast cut to black.

Visits Room, Borstal, packed with visitors. TOM *sits at a table, throwing covert glances around him as he waits. A door's unlocked, instruction issued, door locked again.*
GURVINDER *appears, uniform, shaven-headed, a still-healing slash, ear to mouth, down the side of his face.)*

GURVINDER: (*Sitting; contained; scarcely there*) Hey up, Tom.
TOM: (*Dealing with the face*) How're you doing?
GURVINDER: OK.
    (*Laughter from nearby table.* TOM *takes a look, returns his eyes to the damaged face.*)
TOM: So what happened?
GURVINDER: This? (*Face*) Or this? (*Place*)
TOM: Both. I've been in London doing job interviews, Hester called me . . .
GURVINDER: Yeah, she's bin out t'see us a coupla times, good lass . . .
TOM: She said something about arson . . .
GURVINDER: Yeah. Night o' the Chapeltown riots, two cops swore on a bible they saw me throwin' petrol bombs . . . (*Fingers the cut*) This was a welcoming present from a couple of NFers, Stanley knife, just after I got 'ere . . . Think it suits?
TOM: Christ. This is . . . Did you report it?
GURVINDER: (*A dry laugh*) Oh sure.
    (*Sounds of a woman sobbing.* GURVINDER *flicks a look. More laughter, nearby table.* TOM *studies the new* GURVINDER.)
    D'ye get the job?
TOM: (*Uncertain*) Erm. Matter of fact, I did, yes.
GURVINDER: Good.

TOM: It's . . . erm . . . abroad. Working for the British Council.

GURVINDER: What's that?

TOM: It's to . . . promote the idea of Britain in other countries . . .

GURVINDER: Oh.

TOM: It's just for a year. Before I go up to university or whatever . . .

GURVINDER: Oh. (*Silence.*) I thought your dad had ye down for the
Army or someat.

TOM: My dad's abroad, overseas tour. I'll deal with that when I
have to. It's just for a year or so . . .

GURVINDER: Right.

TOM: Listen, Mona asked me to tell you she's planning a visit next
month, Sandra might come with her . . .

GURVINDER: That'll be nice.

TOM: Wayne I haven't seen. (*Pause*) Or Daisy. She got her A
levels.

GURVINDER: Did she?

TOM: When d'you get out?

GURVINDER: Christmas.

TOM: Will you be all right?

GURVINDER: Oh yeah.

TOM: I left a package of stuff for you at the gate, bits and bobs . . .

GURVINDER: Ta.

TOM: If there's anything else . . .

GURVINDER: I don't think so.
(*Pause.* TOM *glances at his watch.*)
Time is it?

TOM: Quarter to four.

GURVINDER: Is it? (*Pause.*) So.

TOM: Yeah.
(*Pause.*)

GURVINDER: Eh, guess what?

TOM: What?

GURVINDER: In the van comin', guess what I saw through the
window?

TOM: What?

GURVINDER: God's Armchair, five miles.

TOM: Right. Gotscam Chairs . . .

GURVINDER: Yeah.

TOM: Ha.

GURVINDER: Aye. We will do it. When we need to.

    (*A voice lifts, is shushed to stillness.*)

    (*Eventually*) Where ye gonna be workin?

TOM: (*Refocussing*) . . . Jerusalem.

    (*Long pause.* TOM *scans* THE SIKH's *blank-eyed face.*
    Bleed in:)

INSTRUCTOR'S VOICE: Punch, kick, punch. Punch, punch, kick,
    punch . . .

    Slow fade to black.

    Bring up: mug-shot image of Peter Sutcliffe.

    Bring up: HESTER, *in judo gear, at Tai-Kwando class. The
    Instructor calls out small patterns, the class perform them (sound
    effects.).*

INSTRUCTOR: (*Finally*) . . . Punch, punch, kick, kick, punch,
    punch. Rest.

    (HESTER *stands, draws breath, moves to neutral space, bows to
    instructor. Fade Ripper image, bring up black gospel singing, a
    capella opening.*

    Bring up: Image of black Christ on the cross.

    HESTER *steps into the singing, joins it, swinging and clapping
    with the rest as the song gathers momentum.*

    *The singing returns to a capella; underpins what follows on the
    fade.*)

HESTER: (*Jamaican*) I speak for myself, seen? I don't know about
    anybody else. But I don't know how to be British, God
    knows I try and try, but it's not easy and nobody helps. Me
    nah complain – I state the fact. Here is where I'm born, here
    is where I live, here is where I learn, here is where I work,
    here is where I pay my taxes and National Insurance, here is
    where I get my A levels at night school, here is where I study
    accountancy ditto, here is where I'm just another black
    bastard scrounging on the great white British state . . . But
    make no mistake, we Jamaican women strong, we got a
    sisterhood all we own, we nah go nowhere but forward and
    we all go do it together, mek the men them shake them locks

and sing of Abyssinia, we ah go do the work and make the progress, watch we . . . (*Received Standard English*) You see how difficult it is? In Jamaica, no matter how many sentences you start with an 'I' you always fetch up with a 'We'. Maybe it was the same here once, I don't know. But I try. I try to keep to I. I am. I do. I will. I want, I have. I own, I hope. (*Jamaican again.*) But you know, it's a poor tongue you teach we. And a poor tongue pauperizes its people. But see it deh. Peace.
(*She fades.*
Bring up: image of Thatcher.
Bring up: strobe light image:

LASSIE FAIR

SAUNA

MASSAGE

USUAL FACILITIES

Bring up: MONA *washes her hands in cubicle, dries them, presses her buzzer. She wears underwear under a short medical-looking white nylon coat.*)

MONA: (*Out*) . . . Be with you in a minute. (*Turns to deal with arriving client.*) Massage is it, sir? Just lie down, if you would, there we are . . . (*Pours oil on her hands.*) Right, just relax, that's it . . . (*Begins.*) . . . I'm sorry? A menu, yes, I do, what would you like . . .? Well, one hand £10, two hands 15, leather glove 20, topless add 10, tit sandwich 30 . . . No, I don't do that, unhunh, no, you have the list . . . 20? Fine. No, ye pay now. That's right. (*She pockets the money, puts on a leather glove.*) Ye wanna turn over, that's it . . . (*She climbs up on the table, straddles him, sits on his chest, her back to him, facing out. Begins.*) My, look at that, who's a hungry boy them. (*Out, as she does the business.*) What d'ye think? Great, eh? Well, let me tell ye, where I come from it's all 'ands to the pump, if ye'll pardon the expression. All right, first thing, me dad's job goes up in smoke, he's on the dole for the first time since he got here, starts drinkin', can't 'andle it . . . Me brother, right? Steward on the cross-channel boats, gets sent out t'Falklands, does what 'e 'as ter, comes back, two

64

weeks later no job, puff . . . Me mum? Kitchens, General
Infirmary, right? Fifteen years, come hail or come shine.
She's off work, angina, she gets a letter tellin' 'er the
kitchens've bin contracted out, she can apply for 'er old job
with the new lot, but it's fifteen quid less an' more hours . . .
(*To the punter, calm, over her shoulder.*) Don't do that, all
right? (*Goes on with the business.*) Then this nationality law
thing they bring in, suddenly everyone's wonderin' if they've
a right to be 'ere, I was born in fuckin' *Sheffield*, even *I'm*
askin', right? I mean . . . I took two hundred quid nearly last
week. Someone's gotta pay the bills . . . (*She jerks backwards
as the client comes, still takes some of it on her torso.*) There you
go. Very nice . . .
(*She dismounts, hands him towel, wipes herself with another,
peels the glove, presses her buzzer.*)
(*To client*) . . . Sorry, I'd like to, downstairs don't like us
chattin' when there's a queue. Thank you. Come again.
(*Turns out again, washing hands.*) Still, she got back in, didn't
she? So she must be good for someone, right? (*Thinks, shakes
her head.*) You know someat? I find that really scary . . .
(*Turns to new client.*) Massage is it, sir? Just lie down if you
would, that's it.
(*The cubicle slowly fades,* MONA *with it. The Thatcher image
endures.*
Bring in:)

THATCHER'S VOICE: (*Echoic, over*) In the last four years, Britain
has recovered her confidence and self-respect. We have
regained the regard and admiration of other nations. We are
seen today as a people with integrity, resolve and the will to
succeed . . .
(*A sudden downspot lights a large man in Special Response Unit
gear, long perspex shield, long baton, helmet, visor, boots. He
stands motionless, ready to move.*
*Instructor's voice (outdoor acoustic, some distance away) calls the
Advance.*
*The man, in sync with three dozen or so others on the gravel
training ground, takes a ritual step forward, bangs shield with*

*baton. Another call, another identical step forward, until he
arrives, large and menacing, front of stage.
Another call from the Instructor, the men begin rhythmic
banging, batons on shields, voicing victory sounds, yips and
hollers.
A call to stand down, the man relaxes, removes helmet and visor,
laughing and joshing with his mates. It's* WAYNE.
Bring up: The Clash: 'London Calling'. WAYNE *slowly fades.
Bring up: Phonographique, city centre club, throbbing to
Strummer. A mirrored post throws light across the dancers.
The four women out there, dancing it up.* DAISY *wears jeans,
good boots, man's straw hat, 'Coal not Dole' T-shirt;* MONA
wears short white mini, gold rings and chains; HESTER *has a
man's jacket, cord tie and collar, trousers, cuban heels;* SANDRA
*is full Goth, white face, black spiked hair, black eye make-up,
purple lipstick, chains and crosses.
They fade.
Bring up: Michael Jackson: 'Thriller'.
Bring up: downstairs urinal, the music above now perspectived.*
WAYNE, TOM *and* GURVINDER *stand side by side pissing.*
GURVINDER *wears black leather blouson, thick gold necklace,
rings, Armani jeans, baseball shoes;* TOM's *in lightweight suit, a
black and white kuffiah around his neck;* WAYNE *wears pale
slacks and navy blue gold-button blazer, shirt and tie, a police
social club badge sewn on the top pocket.*)

WAYNE: (*Eventually; sodden*) . . . Oh God, I'm fucked.

GURVINDER: Ye will be, come tomorrer, eh, honeymoon boy?

WAYNE: 'Er? Forget it, she's four month pregnant, she don't
wan' it and I don't fancy it . . . No, I mean that last pint's
done my 'ead in . . . Musta bin off.

TOM: (*Deadpan*) Couldn't have been the three Johnny Walkers
you poured in it, could it?
(WAYNE *gives him a leaden look.*)

GURVINDER: (*Climbing stairs to landing payphone*) Up the spout,
eh? Got it.

WAYNE: (*Looking for him*) Whaddya think, ye twat? 'S only
fuckin' reason I'm marryin' 'er . . .

TOM: Does she know that?

(WAYNE *looks at him, uncomprehending*.)

WAYNE: I don't bloody know, do I?

TOM: Just asking.

(WAYNE *zips up, backs out of his stall*. GURVINDER's *on the phone ordering something*.)

GURVINDER: . . . That's right, the Nouveau, nine o'clock, Richards. Yeah . . . and it'll be Miss Patterson, right? And you've got the message . . . Ta . . .

WAYNE: This is my third stag night this week. Come on; I've 'ad enougha this place, where we goin' next . . . ?

GURVINDER: (*Checking Rolex*) Hang on, Duke. We can't leave just yet, got someat lined up for ye . . .

WAYNE: Oh aye? What's that, ye sly bastard? Hope it's a tart . . .

GURVINDER: No fishin', 's a surprise.

TOM: Where've *they* gone, by the way?

WAYNE: (*Staring at him*) What is that, anyway?

TOM: (*Checking* WAYNE's *eyeline*) It's a kuffiah.

WAYNE: Bit puffy, innit? (*To* GURVINDER) You're not thinkin' o' commin' to t'Registry tomorrow in your dad's skirt, are ye . . . ?

(*He laughs. He takes himself in in the mirror, begins exaggerated efforts to smarten himself up*.)

TOM: The women, Wayne.

WAYNE: (*Focussing*) They've gone to the bloody Phonographique, haven't they.

(*Bring up: Siouxsie and the Banshees. Urinal fades.*
Bring up: Phonographique, bar. DAISY *and* SANDRA *sit on stools facing out, their backs to the bar counter, surveying the dance scene in the adjoining room.*

HESTER *looms downstage, jacket and shirt discarded, dancing with style in a thin wool crop top*.)

DAISY: God, Hester's great, isn't she.

SANDRA: Solid. I always wanted to be like her, you know. I don't mean . . . black, I mean solid.

(*She dumps a couple of pills down her throat, chases them with bottled Pils*. DAISY *watches*.)

SANDRA: Ye want?

DAISY: What are they?

SANDRA: Speed. Get you up.

DAISY: I'm fine.

SANDRA: I'm really glad you could come, Daise.

DAISY: Me too, man. You OK?

SANDRA: How d'ye mean?

DAISY: It's what you want . . . ?

SANDRA: Yeah. Dunt everyone?

(DAISY *laughs, orders more Pils.* MONA *arrives, coat on.*)

SANDRA: Oh no, what'd they say, flower?

MONA: Gotta go, job on. I'll see ye back there later, and don't
forget the time, we said we'd get fish suppers in for
t'lads . . .

SANDRA: 'S all right, said I'd show 'em me dress before *he* gets
back . . .

MONA: Yeah, well I've gotta show somebody mine in 'alf an
hour, I 'aven't even put it on, I'd best get me skates on
. . . Where's Miss Goodness?

DAISY: (*Indicating*) Doin' her stuff. What d'ye think? Great,
eh?

(MONA *stares at her sister.*)

MONA: Yeah. If ye like Meccanno, (*To* SANDRA.) Tell 'er I 'ad
t'see a man about a dog. If she notices . . .

(*A look between the two.* SANDRA *kisses her cheek.* MONA
*leaves. The music surges, cuts. Takes up again: Sisters of
Mercy.*

HESTER *cuts out, walks to the bar, sinks her large orange
juice.*)

DAISY: Where d'ye learn t'dance like that, Hes?

HESTER: 'S in the genes. Didn't ye hear? We got rhythm . . .

DAISY: (*Laughing*) Come here, bitch . . .

(*She takes her in her arms, kisses and hugs her off her feet.*)
I'm really glad you came, lovely.

SANDRA: Me too.

HESTER: That makes three of us. But I don't think it gets our
Mona's vote . . . (*Looking.*) She still phoning?

68

SANDRA: No, she's 'ad to go, she'll see us back at her place, she said she was on call tonight . . . (HESTER *frowns a question.*) . . . Pizza Palace. Deliveries.

DAISY: Who was that woman you danced with . . . ? Tall, big eyes . . .

HESTER: Dolly Wardle. She was in 5G . . .

SANDRA: Was that Doris Wardle? Bugger me, I thought it were a dyke in on t'wrong night . . . Dyke Night's Thursdays . . .
(*Pause.*)

DAISY: . . . Don't look unless you're interested, sweetie, but there's a guy making signals at you over there . . .

SANDRA: (*Swinging at once to look*) Oh God, it's Geoffrey Marsden, I owe him fifty quid . . . I'd better go. I'll be back. I hope.
(*She moves off. They sit to watch her. Make giggly signals to her, as she talks and poses.*)

DAISY: Who'd have thought it?

HESTER: What?

DAISY: Sandra a Goth.

HESTER: Oh. Right.
(*A beat or two. They laugh ridiculously, spilling slightly onto each other on their stools.*)

DAISY: And Tom's back.

HESTER: Yes.

DAISY: Be lovely to see him. And Girlie. San said he's been in Manchester . . .

HESTER: Yeah. His folks threw him out, after the Borstal thing.

DAISY: Oh God, really?

SANDRA: (*Arriving*) Is my bag there? (*Finds it.*) I've just got to nip outside a minute, don't go away . . .

DAISY: D'you need anything?

SANDRA: Get us a snakebite, will ye . . . ?

DAISY: ?

SANDRA: Cider and lager . . . I'll definitely be in need o' someat after this . . .

(*She leaves. They watch her go.*)

DAISY: Oh dear. I hope she's not going to do anything *very* foolish.

HESTER: Sandra? No no. Not in her nature. Want to dance?

(*A moment. They laugh again. Move off onto the floor. Dance. They fade. Nouveau, bar. The men sit at a table, watching the scene.*)

WAYNE: . . . I fuckin' love it, boy. I fuckin' love it. I tell you, it's not like a job, it's more like a vocation . . .

GURVINDER: What, like a holiday . . . ?

WAYNE: *Vo*-cation, twat. (*Gurvinder winks at Tom.*) S'like. S'like bein' a priest or a doctor or a . . .

TOM: Estate agent.

WAYNE: Aye, that kinda thing. Ye know, ye walk down the street, people look at you different, automatically give way . . . Finest company of men you'd find anywhere in the land, nothin's too much for a brother officer. Like family, it is. God, look at that pillock there wi' the fuckin' 'air, did ye ever see anythin' like it in your life . . . ? (*Sups his lager.*) Bein' in the force, you know what it's like? It's like playin' for Wales.

GURVINDER: (*Deadpan*) Wow, that good, eh?

WAYNE: That good.

(TOM *looks at his watch.* GURVINDER *gestures to hang on.*)

GURVINDER: How about the women, Duke?

WAYNE: 'Opeless, boy. Can't do the job. Not up to it. Man's work. Good for only one thing, are the women . . .

TOM: What's that, Duke?

WAYNE: You 'avin' me on?

TOM: How'd you mean?

(WAYNE *turns to see who's called him, waves.*)

WAYNE: 'Ey up. Mark, 'ow's it goin' . . . ? (*Watches him move off, waves.*) There's one, salt o' the earth, shoulder to shoulder at Orgreave we were, me an' Mark, oh aye. You don't forget stuff like that . . . (*He dwells on the memory, begins cackling with the pleasure of it.*) Fuckin' Orgreave. Oh boy. I need another piss. When's that bloody surprise comin', our kid, I'm gettin' itchy . . .

GURVINDER: All in good time. What're ye having'?

WAYNE: Pint.

(*He lumbers away.* TOM *watches him go. Looks back at* GURVINDER.)

TOM: He's out of his tree, right?

GURVINDER: How d'ye mean?

(*They laugh.* GURVINDER *strokes the tight bristles of his head, fingers the face.*)

GURVINDER: What d'ye think to it?

TOM: Yeah. Great job.

GURVINDER: Two 'n' half grandsworth.

TOM: On the Health?

GURVINDER: Where've *you* bin? Cash.

TOM: How did you find it?

GURVINDER: I found it. Nuff said.

TOM: So what is it you do?

GURVINDER: This 'n' that. Whatever comes along.

TOM: I thought you wanted to do stand-up . . .

GURVINDER: Did that. Moved on. What about you, how was wheresitsname . . . ?

TOM: Jerusalem.

GURVINDER: Right.

TOM: Extraordinary.

(*Silence.*)

GURVINDER: What? Y'ad a good time . . . ?

TOM: Loved it. Loved it.

GURVINDER: Yeah?

(*Silence.*)

WOMAN'S VOICE: (*Off*) Telegram for Mr Richards . . .

GURVINDER: (*Calling off*) Duke, over 'ere. Surprise time.

(WAYNE *shambles back on.*)

WOMAN'S VOICE: (*Off*) Telegram for Mr Richards, Mr Richards . . .

GURVINDER: (*Calling*) He's 'ere.

(MONA *appears, in abbreviated version of WPC costume, plus stockings, suspenders, boots.* GURVINDER, *huge grin, feeds her on with pointed finger to* WAYNE. *She takes him in. Doesn't find it funny.* TOM *stands, frowns, not party. The buzz of the*

71

room has stilled a little as nearby people ritually watch for the kissogram to unfold.)

WAYNE: Fuck me, Mona Patterson, as I give a heave . . .

MONA: This your idea of a joke, Girlie?

GURVINDER: Aught for a laugh, kid, you know me.

(She looks at Tom, who shakes his head.)

WAYNE: Come on then, cariad, show us yer kecks . . .

(MONA takes out her greetingsgram and a pair of toy handcuffs.)

MONA: 'I come to wish you all the best.

    Tomorrow is your Marriage Test

    And so that Sandra gets some rest

    I hereby place you under arrest.'

(She steps forward, snaps a cuff on WAYNE'*s wrist, the other onto the crossbar of his stool. Laughter, applause from the encircling crowd, as* MONA *holds up the key.)*

Anyone want it?

(She hurls it into the crowd. Leaves.)

WAYNE: Hey. Hey. Ye pillock, what game on . . . ?

(He tries to get up, stumbles, falls over the stool. Thrashes around like a fish in sand. Sound dies.

Bring up: BBC 9 o'clock News intro. music. Lights cut abruptly. Fast plunge up to: DAISY, *crosslegged on floor, face lit by TV, builds a joint in the flickering gleam of the screen.)*

NEWSCASTER: *(Calm, measured)* In the last hour . . .

(He delivers a three-minute headline history of the last five years: tax cuts, unemployment, recession, riots, famine, disaster, privatization, deregulation, growing wealth and poverty, homelessness, urban decay, war, AIDS, law and order, ecology, family values, crime . . . A relentless misericordia, seeding the future, ends of sentences blurring into beginnings, the whole unrelentingly punctuated by reports of the trivial, the frivolous and the mundane (i.e. the Good News). It ends on the September '84 day in question, with news of new hopes of a settlement of the six-month-old Miners' Strike. The last headline begins to fade. DAISY *lights the joint, a WC flushes, lights up on the room, TV out, low hi-fi up.*

HESTER *in from toilet. Joins* DAISY. *Declines joint.)*

HESTER: God, they're going to be all night in there.

DAISY: (*Calling*) Hey, come on, people, we're waiting for the show here.

MONA: (*Off, calling*) Hold your horses, it's got to be right, right?

(DAISY *crawls forward to turn up the music a fraction. Pulls a face as she recognizes Joan Armatrading.*)

DAISY: Who put this on?

HESTER: I did.

DAISY: Joan Armatrading did a *Showbiz for Thatcher* concert.

HESTER: Doesn't make her a bad singer.

DAISY: Come on, she *voted* for the bugger . . .

HESTER: I know. A lot of us did.

DAISY: Get outa here. (*Stares at her.*) You pulling my plonker?

HESTER: (*Giggling*) Maybe.

(DAISY *grabs her, pushes her down, begins tickling her.*)

(*Ecstasy*) Oh no, oh don't, don't do that . . .

(*They roll around on the floor, end up with* DAISY *kneeling astride the pinned* HESTER.)

DAISY: Come on, I want to know, did you or didn't you . . . I'll not let you up.

(MONA *in, looking for something.*)

MONA: . . . I 'ad some pins, somewhere . . . (*Takes them in as she swoops on the discarded joint.*) Hey, you two. Who put this on?

DAISY: Your sister.

MONA: Right. (*Takes her pins. Leaving.*) Nearly there, ladies.

(*She's gone.* DAISY *looks down at* HESTER's *face, stands, legs astride her.*)

DAISY: You know something? (HESTER *shakes her head.*) I could really fancy you.

HESTER: (*Eventually.*) Yeah? What? Are you. A . . . ?

DAISY: Uhunh. I'm overwhelmingly men. You?

(HESTER *gets to her feet, uncertain, dealing with stuff.*)

HESTER: (*Soft*) Get outa here. You having me on?

DAISY: (*Laughing suddenly*) Maybe.

(DAISY *laughs on,* HESTER *eventually joins her, but mutedly.* MONA *in, beating an African drum.*)

73

MONA: Deda. Right. Ladies and gentlemen, please raise your glasses and be upstanding for . . . The Bride, right?
(SANDRA *enters on cue, weirdly wonderful in full length hand-made black velvet dress with half-bustle, bows and matching accessories. They stare at her, stunned.*)

DAISY: (*Coming to*) Wow.

HESTER: Ditto.

MONA: Dunt she look great?

SANDRA: Do you like it?

DAISY: It's

HESTER: Wonderful.

SANDRA: I made it myself.

HESTER: 'S brilliant.

MONA: I did the bows.

DAISY: What does Wayne . . . ?

SANDRA: Hasn't seen it. He'll have to wait till tomorrer.

MONA: Don't want bad luck, right?

DAISY: Right.

SANDRA: (*Speed and love in difficult alliance*) Listen. While we're here. I wanta, I'm really glad you could all, because you're my best friends in all the world and it means a lot to me and because you are my best friends I'm goin' to let you into a secret, well, two secrets really, the first bein' I'm pregnant. I told 'em both on the same day, me dad threw me out and Wayne said 'e'd marry me, two birds with one stone, an' the second bein' I 'ad me fingers crossed all the time 'cos I'm not pregnant at all an' I wanted you to be the first to know . . .
(*She smiles, shy, radiant. The three hug and kiss her in turn.*)
I'm so happy. Aiee. (*She winces as Daisy, last, squeezes her upper arms.*) 'S all right, 's just a bit sore . . . (*The three focus on the heavy bruising on her pale upper arm*) . . . I musta bumped into a door or somethin' . . .
(*A clatter on the stairs,* WAYNE's *voice singing 'Fish and Chips' to the tune of 'Here We Go'.*)

MONA: Goon squad's back, let's be havin' you, San.
(*She ushers her back into the bedroom.*)

DAISY: Bumped into a door?

HESTER: Out of the frying pan . . .
> (*Another huge clatter,* WAYNE *curses,* TOM *and* GURVINDER *struggle in with* WAYNE *supported between them, the toy cuffs dangling from a wrist.*)

GURVINDER: Ladies and gentlemen, pray silence for . . . the Groom.
> (*They stand him carefully up.* WAYNE *sways, focusses, loses it.*)

WAYNE: (*Weird Orville*) I wish I could fly right up to the sky, I wish I could fly. But I can't . . .

GURVINDER: Come on, old son, we'll get your fish 'n' chips . . .

WAYNE: . . . Where's my lovely lady then, my wife-to-be, where's my Sandra gone, are you there mam, dad's 'ome, dada's 'ome, my love . . .
> (*He stumbles across the room and exits for the bedroom, ignoring the women's attempts to dissuade him.*)

GURVINDER: Hey. Look at these two, then.

TOM: Ahunh.

GURVINDER: Don't fancy yours.

DAISY: (*Grinning*) Piss off. Come here.
> (*A crash, a shriek, moans from the bedroom.*)

MONA: (*Lifting*) Wayne! WAYNE! Stop it. Jesus Christ . . .
> (*A heavy heaving sound,* SANDRA *calls out, a long tortured yowl.* MONA *tries to comfort her.*)

HESTER: (*Calling*) Need any help in there?

MONA: (*Off*) No. It's under control.

DAISY: Listen. Somebody should tell them this is a bad idea.

GURVINDER: Good old Daisy.

DAISY: Girlie, I'm serious . . .
> (TOM *begins to giggle, the booze hitting him suddenly.*)

HESTER: What?

TOM: Nothing. I'm supposed to be Best Man, what the hell am I going to *say*? (*He sits on the floor, gazes up at the others.*) It's hardly a marriage made in heaven now, is it? Or Devon, as my grandmother used to say. My deaf grandmother . . .

GURVINDER: I'll feed ye a few jokes, son, ye'll be fine. (*Seeing* MONA *arrive.*) D'ye get the chips in, petal?

(MONA *ignores him, pours herself a glass of wine, lights a cigarette.*)

DAISY: What?

MONA: (*Sitting back*) Oh God, I don't know. Nothin's ever. Right in this world.

(*Silence.*)

GURVINDER: Are they in the oven?

MONA: He walks in, right? She's just took her dress off, he spews up all over it . . . She's heartbroke. He's fast asleep.

(*Silence.*)

GURVINDER: Have ye got any bread, I could murder a chip butty?

DAISY: Oh fuck.

HESTER: All right, so we'll clean it up, what's the problem?

MONA: It's not right. 'S just not right.

DAISY: If I'm her friend I should tell her.

MONA: Tell her what?

DAISY: It's a bad idea. Marrying Wayne.

MONA: Gerroff with ye. She's nuts about 'im.

DAISY: They're wrecks, Mona, both of 'em.

MONA: Who isn't? Nothin' t'do with it.

(*Silence.* GURVINDER *makes a discreet rumbling noise behind his hand.*)

GURVINDER: 'Scuse me. That's my stomach, does that when I'm hungry . . .

MONA: (*Standing, glass in hand*) Right, who wants?

(*All hands go up. She makes to leave.*)

GURVINDER: (*Chuckling*) Eh, you shoulda seen your face down there at the club, our Mona . . . Made Wayne's evenin', did that . . . (*Leans forward to tell the story.*) Ask Tom, he'll tell ye . . .

(MONA*'s reached the wine bottle behind* GURVINDER. *Fills her glass as he rattles on. Slowly pours it over his head. He blinks, splutters, astonished.*)

MONA: (*To group*) Fish 'n' chips?

Lights out.

Music: bring up: the room, the seven, sitting or lying around it,

76

each in separate spots. WAYNE *lies on his face in the centre of the floor, contributes little beyond the occasional groan.*)

SANDRA: Stupid Sandra. Poor old Sandra. Can't help being stupid, that's the way she was born. A victim. A born victim. See it in their eyes, I don't have to look, Daisy, Hester, even Mona. How can they understand? I love me dad. Yes, he's always knocked us around, me mam too 'fore she went to Nottingham, so what, 's how men are, the ones I know anyway. Someat, someat makes men so angry, I don't know what it is, is it me, is it the world? I haven't a clue. Wayne? Most o' the time he's like a big baby, needs mothering, that's all. That's all right. I quite enjoy it. He's gonna buy us a house, the money he earns, specially this year wi' the strike 'n' all. My own house. My own house . . .

HESTER: . . . I go into the vault to reset the timers, he follows me, every morning . . .

SANDRA: . . . I've planned every room. Every one. Furniture. Fabrics. Walls . . .

(*Her light goes out.*)

HESTER: . . . This is the Assistant Bank Manager we're talking about. Sometimes he'll stand really close, behind me, in the vault, I'm working, he's breathing through his nose, sorta smelling me. Then he'll go and stand in one of the bays where he thinks I can't see him and he'll watch me and there'll be this moaning, (*Wayne moans*) low funny sounds coming from him, like a little animal trapped, he thinks I can't see him, his hand's deep in his pocket, deep . . . I mean, this is nine o'clock in the morning, for God's sake . . .

DAISY: Nobody ever grows up nowadays. It's like a collective arrested development . . .

HESTER: . . . I'm this thing. I'm this . . . rubbing post he can't quite reach . . .

DAISY: I have this dream. We're on a cliff, a rock, hundreds of feet up, waiting for something . . .

HESTER: Respect.

TOM: Respect?

HESTER: There's no respect there. I'm this . . . Every morning.
In the vault. Thing . . .
(*Her light goes out.*)

DAISY: . . . It's night. And we're all in kids' clothes, waiting for
something, the bell, the teacher, I don't know. Holding
hands, waiting . . .

MONA: Waitin', right.
(WAYNE *moans again.*)

DAISY: And then. The sun rises. And I wake up. But only in the
dream. I look at the others and they're still asleep, eyes open,
but. Sleeping. Arrested.
(WAYNE *stirs, lifts his head, stares out, lost, returns to oblivion.*)
Nothing signifies any longer. Our eyes never close, we see
everything, but nothing ever means. Menu-time. The post-
modernist rules OK. In a land where everything is
something and nothing is anything. Constructed innocence.
True false rich poor first third winner loser now never me all
fuck wank pick choose be do . . . Menu-time.

GURVINDER: I'm havin' a good time, me . . .

DAISY: I do miss my mum, though.

GURVINDER: I'm doin' all right . . .

DAISY: Before she left – she couldn't stand it here after Greenham
went and . . . (*Long pause*) . . . yeah, and her mum was ill . . .
she left me this note, card, she'd copied out something her
mother had written her years back when she was coming
here . . . (*In Hebrew, then English*) 'Your life is the only truth
you have. And the only truth you need.' Oh God, my
grandmother. She came over to visit once when I was little:
(*Her voice, in heavily accented English*) 'You gotta look in the
pool, Daisy, you understand me, look deep in the pool, what
you see? You see things movin' about, you see things floatin',
mm? Awright. Truth swims. Lies float, awright. Now you
know the difference. . .'

TOM: 'But oh, the difference to me.'

DAISY: So my mum went home. To Israel. Yes, I know. And I'm
on my way up to Sellafield to do a piece for the *Guardian* on

leukaemia-clusters among children living around the plant. And every time I look in the pool I see only me there. Floating.

MONA: Kiting.

DAISY: Not swimming.

MONA: Kiting's what you do like when you've liberated somebody's credit cards, right?
(DAISY's *light out*.)

WAYNE: They wanna lock the bastards up 'n' throw away the key . . .

MONA: Ask Sandra, she's the expert, she kites for Yorkshire, her . . . She's furnished most of her new home by kitin' . . .

TOM: . . . Just please, just let me say, will you, what I have to say and then . . . we can talk.

MONA: I met this bloke, right? I really like 'im. Talkin' to 'im as well. He can talk about all sorts, he can. Anyway, he says what sense is there making a lotta poor people poorer . . . I mean, what d'ye prove by it? Ye can do it? We know that. And get away with it? Do it an' get away with it? Forget it. Ye'll pay. One way or another. Scammin', thievin', kitin', smack, sex, porn. Whatever works. Hands up those'd do different. Try it. Whatever's necessary . . .

TOM: (*Slowly*) I found something there . . . Dad. Mum. That . . . not . . . how to . . .

MONA: That's what *he* says, anyway. Trouble is, 'e's a fuckin' Rasta. 'E'd want to call the girl baby Ethiopia or someat. Meself, I like Tamsin. What d'ye think to Tamsin? Tamsin Patterson. Tamsin Patterson. Tamsin. (*She pats her stomach: an echo.*) Tamsin? (*Whispers.*) Can you hear me? Tamsin? (*Giggles.*) It's your mum . . .

TOM: Dad . . .

MONA: (*Whisper, light fading*) It's your mother, Tamsin. (*She's gone.*)

TOM: Oh fuck it, I'll write. I can't *tell* them, there's no language, they think I'm nuts as it is, gone native or too much sun or something. I start talking about history and . . . culture and language and *people*, they'll send for a doctor. Jesus, I'm not

even sure I can explain it to myself. I've had my name down
for Sandhurst since I was three. I learnt to salute before I
learnt to shake hands. My country, right or wrong. Mean
and cunty. Cadet-speak . . . (*Takes off his kuffiah*) The child
who gave me this. In Ramallah. On the West Bank. Under
military occupation and ruled by decree. In violation of
international law. Who lost the whole of his immediate
family in the massacre at Sabra el-Shatila. Father, mother,
two sisters, four brothers. Where three thousand-odd
Palestinians, men, women, kids, babies, ancients, were
systematically shot and clubbed to death street by street and
shack by shack by Christian militiamen. While the Israeli
military sealed the camps up against escape or rescue.
Showed me, the boy who gave me this, more affection, more
respect, more grace, more of what it is to be human than
anything in my life here has ever prepared me for. At home.
Or anywhere else . . .

WAYNE: (*Unbudging*) Talk about the enemy within! Oh boy!

TOM: Do not teach me what to feel.
Until you are able first to teach me how.
When you weave me into your life
Do not tie off the thread.
You have travelled the world
And seen only England there.
I have been among old souls
For whom two hundred years is like
A single day and two thousand miles
A single stride . . .

GURVINDER: Fuck 'em.

TOM: Listen, fuck it. I'll write.
(*Light out.* GURVINDER *sits, blowing gently on steepled fingers,
lips moving darkly towards meaning.*)

GURVINDER: Fuck 'em. I'm a king, me. (*He looks around the
room.*) Wayne, you awake? Wayne? (*Toes him in the ribs. He
moans.*) The package, Wayne, ye got it?

WAYNE: (*Not moving; tapping the blazer he's wearing.*) Jacket.
(GURVINDER *kneels into* WAYNE's *downlight, feels the blazer,*

*fishes a brown manila envelope from inside pocket, examines
contents, opens and studies a typewritten invoice, stows it into his
coat, takes out a roll of fifties, peels eight, folds them, fixes them
to the back of* WAYNE's *jacket collar with a paper clip. Sits back
in his chair. Broods.*
Light out.
Silence.
WAYNE *slowly struggles up to hands and knees, the notes on his
neck. Stares out.)*

ACT TWO

WAYNE, *in summer uniform, smokes a fag and chews gum in a corridor. Sounds of trial in nearby courtroom.*

WAYNE: (*Out*) You won't want to know about Orgreave Coking Plant, will you? No no. A squeamish people, we are. We act ashamed of some of our greatest triumphs. Well let me tell you, the war was won because the battle of Orgreave was won. And Orgreave was won because the High Command – I don't mean policemen either, I mean Upstairs – because the High Command decided that's where we'd stand and fight, got it? (*Deliberately.*) By any means necessary. That was the words used. Nearly five thousand of us mustered down there, from all over the place, I'd no idea where some of 'em came from, Hampshire, where's Hampshire . . .? Two hundred horses, a hundred dogs, four hundred long shields, five hundred short shields, protective gear from visored helmets to steel-cap boots, oh yes, planned and executed with military precision, we 'ad a hundred and fifty paras in unmarked police boiler suits, two buses filled with fuckin' CS gas, that's how serious they were Upstairs . . . We were there to beat the shit out of 'em that day an' by God that's what we did. Hey, I watched one o' the mounted boys chase a gang o' pickets into the fuckin' Asda down the village, follered 'em inside . . . (*Laughs*) An' the fuckin' Met, oh boy, my mate Mark saw the boys from the Met charging down the High Street smashin' in every car windscreen with an NUM sticker, hundreds of 'em, with a couple o' lads followin' up with a little printed card for the wiper, Mark showed me one: 'Congratulations. You have met the Met.' There's pride, is it. The really comical thing is, the poor bastard pickets 'adn't come for a bundle at all, they thought it was gonna be business as usual, you know, shove an' heave when the lorries moved the coke out an' a bit of a laugh after . . . Most of 'em were in T-shirts 'n' daps, you know, trainers . . .

Didn't know what hit 'em. We followed through, too. Oh yes. We had men scourin' the hospitals all night, draggin' the wounded out 'n' bangin' 'em up, we did. An' a brand new charge to throw at the buggers too, them we arrested: riot. Carries a life sentence, see. Exemplary. Upstairs again. Oh yes. (*His name's called. He drops the fag, treads it out.*) We've been months stitchin' this lot up – I didn't write a fuckin' word o' my statement, I don't think anybody did, 's all bin taken care of, see . . . (*Points: Upstairs, Grins. His name's called again.*) A riot, eh?
(*He saunters forward to the witness box. Chews on as he takes the oath.*)

DEFENCE COUNSEL: (*Off*) . . . I appear for the defendant Ian Clayton. Now, Constable Richards, since you have made out your Statement to this Court as Arresting Officer all those many months ago – you have a copy of your statement . . . ?

WAYNE: Yep.

COUNSEL: (*Off*) . . . As I say, since last . . . December, when you signed your Statement of Evidence, we have had the good fortune to learn of the existence of a continuous video record of the day's events taken by the Police Authorities themselves. And the court in its wisdom has allowed the defence to have the whole of that recording admitted as evidence in this trial. Now, what I'd like to do, Constable Richards, as I have done with your colleagues from the Assistant Chief Constable down, is to take you through your sworn statement, step by step, in the light of what the objective police record of those same events has to tell us . . .
(*A monitor throws garish light on* WAYNE*'s face. He turns a little to stare at it.*)

COUNSEL: (*Off*) Are you chewing gum, Constable?

WAYNE: I am. (*Takes it out.*) Musta forgot it.

COUNSEL'S VOICE: (*Off; on the fade*) You'll see, top right corner, the time code. We'll begin at 12 noon, the time at which, according to your statement, the short shields moved out to clear the men on the bridge . . .

WAYNE: (*Out again: screen still bright*) Can you imagine? We've

got the buggers stitched up fair 'n' square 'n' then we let 'em
see a *police* recording of what actually went *down* . . . ? Dear
God, what a cock-up eh? . . . Dear dear dear . . .
(*Trail car radio news: UN says 19 million Africans face famine;
Poll Tax to start in 1990; Water to be privatized; 278 AIDS-
related deaths in Britain; hole in the ozone layer above the
Arctic . . .*
Bring up: GURVINDER, *lancing down M62 in big car, tapping
out number on phone. Radio out as he connects.*)
GURVINDER: Sidney? Mr K. You got your pad? OK, the six
houses in Peckham, yes? Buy 'em, I'll send you the names
for the mortgages. Ahunh. No, I think it's right, ye can smell
it a mile off . . . (*Listens*) Listen, I'm off to Manchester about
that other thing . . . peashooters, right. (*Laughs*) I'll let you
know. There's a market, don't worry. They demand, I
supply. I rest my case . . .
(*He laughs, listens a moment, hangs up, drives on.*
Bring up, underneath:)
MONA: You're not.
SANDRA: I am.
(*Lights up on the women, both on the phone.*)
MONA: You're not.
SANDRA: I am.
MONA: 'S amazin'. So am I.
SANDRA: You're not.
MONA: I am.
SANDRA: You're not.
(*They laugh.*)
It's not . . . ?
MONA: I think so, yeah. Hey, what did Wayne say?
SANDRA: He said: Oh aye? Where've I 'eard that one before?
MONA: (*On the fade*) He didn't? Bastard.
SANDRA: (*On the fade*) He bloody did.
(*Lights out.*
Bring up: DAISY, *rehearsing piece to camera from autocue;
invisible Make-Up bobs in and out, doing her eyes in breaks.*)
DAISY: 'Whatever bland reassurances are to come out of the

Ministry of Agriculture, the facts are bleak and inescapable: the world's worst nuclear disaster has sent a huge wave of radioactive contamination across the farmlands of North Yorkshire and the cost to the lives of the people who work them will be enormously high . . .' (*Peers at autocue*) . . . Is that it? Where's the link passage for the Kirkstall piece? (*Puts cans on.*) Anyone there? Charles, is Charles there . . . ? (*To Make-Up*) Easy with that one, I've an infected follicle . . . (*Back to mike again*) Charles, the link to the Kirkstall piece . . . it's what? Wait a minute, are you telling me . . . Listen, fuck the Head of Local Programmes, fuck ITN, we have a stream in the middle of Leeds registering a bequerel-count of several squillions and you're telling me they don't want it . . . ? So it was a CND group took the reading, you think they're less reliable than the Ministry of Agriculture for God's sake? . . . So it's out. I see.
(*Long pause. She stands there a long time dealing with it. Removes the cans. Angles for the make-up again.*
Crossfade to MONA, *watching TV, swaddled infant asleep at her tit.* Neighbours *end titles. She clicks sound off, looks at kid. Gently eases mouth from nipple. Lays kid down to sleep at her side. Returns to her exercise book and pencil. The kid stirs.*)

MONA: (*Jamaican; the first time*) This is for you, all right? When you is old enough to read, like a diary, but not all the days, 'bout all the things that did happen while you was still inside me, seen? Like ahhmm . . . (*Flicks pages*) . . . You wahn me read you some eh? Hear dis. 'Friday June 26th. Me did get the results dis morning and you is a girl. I been really happy all day, knowing. What you think of Jojo for a name? Or Marva? Me no sure. I gwahne work extra hard you see so that we can have a chance of being happy together and not down in poverty an' . . . (*Screws up nose*) Is that how ye spell poverty . . . ? (*She's not sure, works on it, Phone rings. She picks up. In English.*) Hello. Oh, hello, Bluesie. What? Oh no, I'm feedin' the bab. (*Listens.*) Yeah, an' what does 'e want? Ahunmh. No, it'd need to be twenty. OK, put 'im on.

85

(*She checks the bab. The guy comes through.*) Miss Birch here,
I understand you've been a very naughty boy . . . Well,
you'd better tell me about it and then we'll decide what
we're going to do with you . . . Ahunh. Speak up, speak
up . . .
(*She lays the phone down, gathers the babe, lays her in
carrycot. The client burbles on. Fade.*
Bring up: effects, a number being dialled.
Bring up: a Flight-Simulator (screen). TOM, *in RAF drabs, at
game control-panel, landing a plane as he waits for the phone to
pick up. Gets engaged signal. Lights up.*
Bring up: GURVINDER, *car phone, on the road again, speaking
with his money manager.*)
GURVINDER: . . . TSB, I can do twenty thou, British Gas fifty.
Thou, twat. I'll get you the names, don't worry, it's a big
family . . . (*Laughs*) No, but I know a guy who does.
Sidney, the houses in Streatham, make it eight, I'm tekin' a
bundle over in Manchester and I need somewhere to put it
. . . Fine, call me back.
(*Phone down. He drives, palming his cropped head with one
hand. Phone.* TOM's *light up as* GURVINDER *collects it.*
Mr K. Tom, ye bugger, how've ye bin, are ye back . . . ?
TOM: Yeah, I'm in London, Girl –
GURVINDER: Yeah? What're ye doin'?
TOM: This 'n' that. Thinking of getting into hi-tech . . . Listen
Girlie, I just got off the phone from Hester . . .
GURVINDER: Haven't seen her in months, how is she . . . ?
TOM: . . . There's bad news, Girlie . . .
GURVINDER: . . . Hang on, Tom, porkers . . .
(TOM's *light out.*
GURVINDER *pulls into the middle lane, the chasing police
Rover whooshes by at 120. He watches them a moment, takes
out an imaginary pistol, aims, fire, the gun bucks in his hand,
he mouths the sounds of the Rover screaming out of control and
careering off the motorway: a chill moment. Returns to call.*
. . . OK, Thomas, you give me the bad news. I'll give ye
the good . . . (*Listens*) You're kiddin'. Dead? I don't . . . I

was over there a coupla weeks back . . . (*Hears worse*) Oh,
fuck, no . . . No.
(*He deals with it in silence, listening on. Lights out.*
Bring up: SANDRA *in downspot, kneeling, blissed out, a baby-*
bundle in her arms.
SANDRA: (*Singing*) . . . A kiss for the baby
    The newly born baby
    A kiss for the baby
    Now giv'n to the Lady . . .
(*She repeats it, on and on, as if singing a round, bleaching it of*
meaning. Stops suddenly. Stares at the bundle. Loses interest.
Lets it drop from her arms.)
I wanted to call him Timothy but Wayne said it 'ad to be
Arfon after his dad. I like Timothy, I don't know why.
Anyway. Eleven months, I don't think he didn't cry more
than two nights, used to break my heart, leave him, let him
learn, says Wayne. How can you? How can you? Anyway. I
used to wait until Wayne was asleep and then go in and lift
him till he stopped. Anyway, this night he just cries and
cries, I took him down in the kitchen to give him some pobs,
Wayne comes chargin' down an' tells me to put 'im back in
his cot an' I won't an' he tries to take 'im from me an' I won't
let go an' he just goes crazy, just goes crazy, drags the boy
away from me and just throws him. Just throws him.
(*Silence.*) Everyone's bin really nice. I've bin stoppin' at
Mona's an' Girlie's looked after a lotta things an' I 'ad a really
nice card from Hester an' Daisy came an' . . . (*Silence.*) I
don't really blame Wayne, he'd 'ad a lot on 'is plate they'd
just passed 'im over for promotion an' Wales'd lost again . . .
Four years, they gave him, manslaughter. (*Silence.*) I don't
know who I do blame. I don't. (*Sings.*) A kiss for the baby
(*Long pause.*) The newly born baby (*Long pause.*) A kiss for
the baby.
(*Slow fade to black.*
Bring up: Sounds of breakfast TV spraying headlines for '87;
Zeebrugge, King's Cross, October hurricane, Bangladesh floods,
Black Thursday, Enniskillen, end of Wapping, Hungerford, ten

million HIV-positive world-wide, 90 per cent ozone layer
depletion over Antarctica.
Bring up: HESTER, *in spot, at doorway of mum's bedroom. She's*
fastening a short Crimplene housecoat over her dove-grey business
suit and white silk shirt.)

HESTER: . . . Now you sleep on, Mama. Doctor'll be here at
twelve, no need for you to stir, Hester's home. (*She peers in,*
smiles at the already dozing mother. Soft.) That's right. (*Looks*
out again. Quoting, mother's voice.) 'When Mona want help,
she call Mama. When Mama want help, she call Hester.
That's the way it is, child. I know my girls . . .' I know my
girls, mm? The girls we were, maybe. Not the women we
are. Sometimes I ache to tell her. When she says: you got a
boyfriend yet, Hester girl? Sure I got a boyfriend, mama, she
called Joan, we livin' in sin in Peckham . . . It's all right,
nobody knows, you're the first to be told. I'm not ready for
the world to know my business just yet. Imagine. (*Thinks.*)
You know, I wonder sometimes how Mona explained Jojo
and . . . (*Dwells, blanking the rest out.*) . . . the rest. Whatever
it is. OK. Let's get this deregulated dream of a day on the
road.
(*Bring up lights, as she moves into the Patterson living room,*
gathers a plastic basket of washing for the washroom.)

MONA: (*Off*) Hi. It's me, mama . . . (*Appearing*) Ye there, mama?
(*Sees Hester. Mona has Jojo's carrycot in her hands. They stare*
at each other.)

HESTER: She's having a lie-in.

MONA: What're you doin' up 'ere?

HESTER: I got a few days off . . .
(*Mona lays carrycot on sofa, shakes rain from hat.*)
(*Lays basket down*) . . . Drove up last night.

MONA: Ye got a car, have ye? (*Hester nods.*) Is Mum OK?

HESTER: She's just tired. Called me yesterday.

MONA: Why the hell she call you in London, I'm quarter of an
hour away?

HESTER: 'When Mama need help, she call Hester . . .' You want
coffee?

(MONA *shakes her head.* HESTER *crouches over the cot to take a look at Jojo.*)

MONA: An' who does Hester call?

HESTER: God, she's grown. (*Stands.*) Hester stands on her own two feet.

MONA: Lucky Hester. I'll look in on Mum . . .

HESTER: Don't wake her.

MONA: Look. I've arranged to leave the kid, I'm tekin' Sandra over to Hull to see Wayne . . .

HESTER: It's in hand. I'll look after her.

(MONA *frowns, uncertain.*)

How's she coping? Sandra.

MONA: She's all right. She's waitin' in t'car.

HESTER: You've got a car?

MONA: Some 'opes. Girlie laid it on. (*Hands her the carrier bag.*) That's her grub an' nappies 'n' stuff. I'll just tek a look . . .

(*She leaves for the bedroom.* HESTER *methodically unpacks the bag, checks and organizes the gear: food; nappies; books and toys.*

SANDRA *wanders in. She's pale, pinched, nervy beneath the supinity. Watches a moment, as* HESTER *turns to study the sleeping Jojo.*)

SANDRA: She's lovely, in't she?

HESTER: (*Seeing her*) Hello, San. How are you?

SANDRA: I'm fine thanks.

(HESTER *hugs her to her.* SANDRA *begins to flake, though not to tears.*)

HESTER: Oh love, what a nightmare, what a . . .

SANDRA: Can't be 'elped. God musta wanted it. We're gonna see Wayne, ye know about . . . ?

HESTER: Yes I do.

SANDRA: He's havin' a horrible time, him bein' a copper . . . ex . . . an' what 'e did, like . . . they've 'ad to put 'im in with all the perverts 'n' that.

(*Silence. She shivers, rubs her arms.*)

I came in for a wee.

HESTER: (*Indicating*) Help yourself. Mona's in with mum.

(SANDRA *heads off, returns for her handbag, leaves.* HESTER *makes to go to the bedroom, stops as she becomes aware of* MONA *and mother in low-toned chat.*)

(*Removing housecoat*) Mona, don't you tire her now.

(*The phone rings. She searches the room for it, unearths it from inside her mother's wicker sewing-basket.*)

(*Phone*) Hester Patterson . . . Hello, beauty . . . Of course I'm up, I just couldn't find the phone, mother hates it, she hides the damn thing . . . You get my note? Yes. I'm sorry too. No, she's just a bit fragile, she'll be OK . . .

(MONA *returns to the room. Listens, unseen, to the call, though wholly without guile, stroking the discarded housecoat as she does so.*)

(*Phone*) . . . Three or four days. I've got a business to run . . . well, *we* have. (*Laughs at the response.*) It's true, man. Time, tide and Financial Services wait for no girl . . . Hey, don't start talking dirty, it's early morning, I have a child to tend and people all over the flat . . .   (*Laughter. Answer*) I'm wearing my power suit, that's what I'm wearing . . . (*Answer*) Never *mind* . . . (*Straight*) Yeah, you too. Mmm. Mmmmm. Call you later. Yeah.

(*Phone down. She stands a moment, deep in it, turns, sees* MONA.)

MONA: Fuck me.

HESTER: What?

MONA: Ye could do that for a livin', ye know that? (*Laughs, a touch brittle.*) I guess ye don't 'ave to.

HESTER: Does anybody?

(*Silence.*)

MONA: What's this about you inviting our mum to go 'n' live with ye down south?

HESTER: What's your problem, Mona?

MONA: What d'ye mean?

HESTER: I am *not* an outsider here, OK? And I don't have to answer to you or anyone else for what I say or don't say to my *mother* . . .

MONA: . . . I didn't say ye did . . .

HESTER: Don't worry, you're not going to lose your child-minder and general factotum, Mum's too daft about Jojo to even consider it . . .

MONA: God, you're a stuck-up bitch, though . . . With your fucking car and your 'power suit' an' your own fuckin' business, a real little Tory, a real little black Brit, right?

HESTER: What I do is my affair, child . . .

MONA: Don't child me, sweetheart . . .

HESTER: . . . You need to take a look at yourself one of these days . . .

MONA: Oh do I? 'S all comin' out, is it? Come on then, let's have it.

HESTER: Oh, go on about your business, will you. Another time.

MONA: Fine. Anytime's fine by me.
   (*A short fume of unreleased anger hovers between them.* HESTER *turns to the stack of kid's stuff on the table, needing process.*)
   D'ye know what to do?

HESTER: Yes, I know what to do.

MONA: Ask mama if ye're stuck. I'd best get off, Sandra'll be . . .

HESTER: (*Bathroom*) Sandra's in there.
   (*Silence.*)

MONA: She's what?

HESTER: Yes, she came in earlier, while you . . .
   (MONA *rushes past her. Bangs on bathroom door, off.*)

MONA: (*Off*) Sandra! Sandra, you all right? *Sandra* . . .
   (*Sounds of lavatory flushing.* SANDRA *wanders back into the room, smiling, blissed out.*)

SANDRA: I needed a wee . . .

MONA: (*Still off.*) Oh God, Sandra, what are you doing to yourself, girl?
   (*She returns to the room, Sandra's bliss gear in her hands.*)
   . . . How in God's name are you gonna tell Wayne ye're leavin' 'im wi' this lot inside ye?

SANDRA: I'm fine. I'm fine. Feelin' mmm fine.

MONA: Here, tek your bag, get in the car.

SANDRA: (*Perching*) Tek me home. I don't want to go to Hull. He just makes me depressed.

MONA: Oh San, we've bin thro' all this, love, ye said ye'd tell 'im . . .

SANDRA: I'll tell 'im. I'll tell 'im.
(*She gets up, begins leaving.*)
Thanks for your card, Hes. It was very kind.

HESTER: I'll call and see you before I go.
(SANDRA *floats out.*)

MONA: Why didn't ye tell me she was in there?

HESTER: I didn't *know* . . . Jesus.

MONA: No. I bet ye didn't. Not your business to, is it?
(*She crosses to look at Jojo, adjusts a blanket, rises.*)
Feed 'er soon as she wakes, will ye? . . . Beef 'n' carrot.
(*She leaves.* HESTER *follows to the window, watches her leave the building for the car.*
MRS PATTERSON *starts to sing in the bedroom: 'How Great Thou Art', low, rhythmic, though the breathing's difficult.* HESTER *listens, still watching. Her hips slowly sway with the song.*)

HESTER: Not my business. I am. I do. I have. I own. I win. I lose.
(*The hips stop.*) My business. How great thou art.
(*Lights out.*
Bring up: Radio One gunge, shot through with pop radio news headlines driving through '88: Salmonella, Lockerbie, Piper Alpha, Clapham Junction, GCHQ sackings, Lawson budget [four top tax rates abolished], charges for eye tests, dental treatment, Clause 28 . . .
Beneath, lifting towards the end, a car-phone beeps out a number, waits for pick-up.
Fade up: GURVINDER, *parked, staring intently out at something as he waits, phone to ear.*
Radio out. Ringing tone continues.
Bring up: sounds of Dales countryside; a bright day. The phone's answered.)

MAN'S VOICE: (*Phone; in Punjabi*) Hello, who's speaking please?

GURVINDER: Dad, it's Gurvinder. (*Silence. In English.*) Can we talk, please . . .? I need to talk, Dad . . .

(*Receiver goes down.* GURVINDER *deals with it. Eventually buttons Redial. Ringing tone for some while.*)

WOMAN'S VOICE: (*Punjabi*) Hello, who is it, please?

(GURVINDER *bites his lip, unable to speak. She repeats the question twice; he hangs up.*

GURVINDER *stares out again. Birds sing. He finds he's weeping. Sniffs. Wipes his eyes. Pads out a number.*)

GURVINDER: (*Phone*) Sidney. Mr K. Mr K. I'm OK, I've got a cold. The houses, Sidney. Sell 'em. No, all of 'em. I smell the end, kid, the rising curve has risen, enough's enough, kill or be killed, winners and losers, there is no alternative, markets maketh man, you hearing me? (*Sniffs*) The Club Opening, Sidney. No, the one in Leeds. I've had an idea. Midsummer Night. June sometime, look in a fuckin' calendar, how would *I* know? And listen, clear your diary for it, I may need you up here hosting, I've other plans for the night, I'll let ye know . . .

(*Hangs up. Stares out again, eyes intent on something in the distance. Behind him, the distant shimmering image of Malham Cove slowly registers on the screen.*

Lights down. The image and GURVINDER's *rapt face persist for some moments. Fade.*

Bring up: Exterior flashing neon sign: The Shining Path.

Music: Betty Boo, or worse, from inside, half drowned in the din of the opening night rave.

Bring up: DAISY, *forecourt, speaking on cordless. She wears shorts, trainers, T-shirt with* Vote Donald *on the front,* Democracy is a Dead Duck *on the back.*)

DAISY: (*Through*) . . . Hey, Girlie, it's Daisy, what's going on, where's everyone . . . ? No, I'm outside, waiting. No, I don't want to come in, ye've seen one club opened, ye've seen 'em all . . . (*To comment from passing peckerhead.*) You never seen legs before, arsehole? Yeah, up yours too. (*Back to phone.*) No, some passing peckerhead. So how long you gonna be? And Tom and Hester's train's when? Ahunh. Ahunh.

GURVINDER *appears from club, phone to ear, talking quietly.*

He wears shades, lightweight silk suit, Shining Path *pitcher's cap. Fetches up next to her, a couple of strides away.*

. . . Hang on, you're breaking up, I can't hear a fucking word you're saying . . .

GURVINDER: Can you hear me? Hello. Hello.

(*She angles the phone, eventually sees him.*)

DAISY: You twat.

GURVINDER: (*Pulling her in to him*) Hey, Dais, look at you. You look great, wow, mm.

DAISY: Enough, I came already. What's this, your second million?

GURVINDER: Who's countin'? Shall we go?

DAISY: Go where? What is this Magical Mystery Tour crap?

GURVINDER: First we collect Tom and Hester. After which, in the fullness of time, all will be revealed . . .

DAISY: No way. I need at least a clue.

GURVINDER: A clue? Ten years.

DAISY: That's a clue?

GURVINDER: Trust me. When did I ever let you down?

DAISY: What, apart from the rave-up down the drift-mine, the balloon trip, the . . .

GURVINDER: (*Taking her arm*) Ye're growing old, chick. Trust me. First the station, next the world . . .

(DAISY *swings a kick at his arse as they leave for the car. Music surges. Segues into Talking Heads: 'We're on the Road to Nowhere'.*

Lights out.

Bring up: car sounds, on the move in the dark. [*All voices off*])

DAISY: A *Bentley*, Girlie. Gross.

HESTER: Really.

GURVINDER: (*Chuckle*) I know.

(*Car slowing, feeling its way.*)

TOM: So where the hell are we?

GURVINDER: Almost there.

HESTER: Almost where?

GURVINDER: Trust me.

TOM: Midsummer madness, Hes.

94

DAISY: Urgh. A drinks cabinet.
  (*Brake. Silence. Sounds of deep country.*)
HESTER: What?
  (*Car door.*)
GURVINDER: Base camp. Let's get the gear . . .
  (*Car doors.*)
DAISY: Gear? What gear?
  (*Bring up: Improvized camp-site, moonlit, deep in the country, a
  canvas awning, picnic table, hampers of food, booze, sleeping
  rolls, linen basket, lamps slung around the space.
  GURVINDER sits crosslegged in the mouth of the awning,
  checking and setting an old-fashioned alarm clock.
  TOM is carrying brushwood; begins lighting the fire he's been
  preparing. He wears an ancient leather flying jacket, a funky
  Biggles leather helmet.*)
TOM: 'S that?
GURVINDER: Just in case.
TOM: Right.
GURVINDER: Be a night to remember, will this.
TOM: I can't say I've forgotten the night of the drift mine.
  Partying in four feet of flood water with the 1st Squadron
  Hell's Angels tends to stick in the mind . . .
GURVINDER: Yeah yeah. Ye'll see.
  (*He stands, joins TOM at the fire. Gazes up at the sky. TOM
  stands, wipes his hands.*)
TOM: So where are we exactly?
GURVINDER: Close.
  (*They look at each other. GURVINDER's eyes rage in the
  darkness.*)
TOM: (*Quiet, drawn*) You're really wired, aren't you?
GURVINDER: Na. You know me. (*He grins*) So how ye bin?
TOM: Fine.
GURVINDER: (*Eyes strong again*) Have ye? (*TOM turns away,
  uneasy, jabs at the fire.*) Still in . . . what was it? hi-tech?
TOM: Yeah. Still in hi-tech.
GURVINDER: So that thing abroad was just er . . .
TOM: Filling in, yeah.

(GURVINDER *crouches at the fire.*)

GURVINDER: Shame. (*Beats*) You're not *with* Hester, are ye?

TOM: (*Refocussing*) Hester? No. Why?

GURVINDER: I'm thinkin' of asking 'er to marry me.

TOM: What? (GURVINDER *grins, points a teasing finger at him.*) Fuck off.

GURVINDER: Come on, I'ad ye goin', right? 'S right, innit?

TOM: (*Pleased*) Same old Girlie.

(HESTER *and* DAISY *in, wet from tarn, borrowed swimsuits, towels.*)

HESTER: (*To* TOM) The man wasn't lying, Tom. He's only laid on a mountain lake . . .

DAISY: (*Crouching behind him on his shoulders.*) Come on, Biggles, tell us what you know, what's he up to?

TOM: (GURVINDER's *sounds.*) He's sayin' nowt, 'im.

DAISY: (*Pushing him*) All men together, eh?

TOM: (*Falling, laughing*) It's true, it's true . . .

HESTER: Will somebody at least put me out of my misery? Is our Mona coming . . . ?

GURVINDER: 'S possible.

HESTER: Oh great.

DAISY: How about San?

GURVINDER: San's movin' around. On the road. Took off in spring. She knows, though. I'm in touch.

TOM: What about Wayne, anyone been to visit . . . ? (HESTER *and* DAISY *shake heads.*) Me neither . . .

GURVINDER: (*Sudden, in the silence*) I 'ave.

(*They look at him. His eyes burn a little.*)

TOM: How is he?

GURVINDER: He's missed ye.

HESTER: (*After thought*) I'm sorry, I can't deal with Wayne, not after . . .

DAISY: (*Scanning him*) What're you up to, King . . . ? You gonna let us in on . . . ?

(GURVINDER *swings suddenly away, scents the air, a night animal.*)

GURVINDER: (*Fast*) Sh.

96

(*They listen. Bleed in sound of distant motor-bike.*)

DAISY: What? What?

GURVINDER: (*Slow uncoil*) 'S OK. 'S on the top road.

DAISY: Jesus, you looked like James Cagney there for a
    minute . . .

GURVINDER: (*Perfect James Stewart*) Wa, tha's the way it is,
    sweetheart.

HESTER/DAISY: (*As one*) That's James Stewart.

DAISY: (*Lighting joint*) Wanker. (*Through held breath.*) Listen, can
    we at least eat, please? I'm famished . . .

GURVINDER: There's some nibbles, salmon mousse 'n' shit . . .

HESTER: Hey, you froze just then, man. Is any of this illegal, I
    mean you're not expecting the police or anything? It'd be
    nice to know.

DAISY: (*Half-hearing*) The cops? Where?

    (GURVINDER *swings round again to look out at the dark. Sounds
    of car approaching, slowing, headlamps scoring their space as it
    stops.*)

    (*Finding tin in her bag*) Oh shit. It's the cops.

    (Silence. GURVINDER *moves forward carefully, eyes on the car.
    Behind him,* DAISY'*s busy emptying contents of tin into a party
    bag of crisps. The headlamps suddenly dip, flood back, dip
    again, die.*)

GURVINDER: (*Jive, flicking fingers*) All right! (*He moves back
    towards the awning.*)

DAISY: Fuck. That's all my mushrooms gone . . .

GURVINDER: We don't need 'em, Dais. Trust me.

MONA: (*On the approach*) . . . I'm in a field full o' cowshit in the
    middle of nowhere at midnight, right, this better be good,
    Gurvinder. I've come straight from work for this . . .

    (*She struggles in, tight mini, heels, sleeveless white vest and
    African shawl.*)

MONA: Thank God, I thought I'd got the wrong mountain for a
    minute . . .

    (*They crowd round, greetings, hugs, sprays of chat, a surge of
    new energy.*)

    Hey, guess who picked me up in Girlie's limo? (*To

GURVINDER) Have ye told 'em . . . ? (GURVINDER *shakes his head*.) You'll never guess.

TOM: Nigel Mansell.

MONA: I'm serious.

DAISY: Oh right. Prince Charles. Teddy Kennedy?

MONA: Listen, I'm serious . . .

(WAYNE *appears behind her, in blue chauffeur's jacket, peaked cap; stops on the edge of their space*.)

HESTER: (*Disbelieving*) Wayne?

(MONA *frowns, follows their eyes, sees him*.)

WAYNE: (*Uncertain; small*) Hiya. (*Beat*.) Nice to see you all again.

(*No one speaks.*

He looks at the Gladstone bag in his hand, scans the site for signs of GURVINDER.)

Just brought this up for the Chief. I'll not stop if . . .

MONA: (*Aware of the group*) I don't mind, Wayne.

HESTER: (*Low*) Speak for yourself.

MONA: I do.

(TOM *gets up, comes towards him*.)

TOM: How've you been, Duke?

WAYNE: Oh, so so, you know. You?

TOM: Much the same really.

DAISY: Hello, Wayne.

WAYNE: Hiya, Daise.

MONA: I thought 'e were comin' out next month.

WAYNE: No, this.

(*He looks at* HESTER. *She moves in*.)

HESTER: I've got a lot of bad feelings towards you, Wayne, sorry. Stuff I've got to deal with . . .

WAYNE: I know. Me too.

(*Silence, unease still hovering.*)

MONA: Oh, this is gonna be fuckin' *great*, I shoulda gone to me bed . . .

(*A high, amplified sound from the awning swivels them upstage. They focus eventually on the ghetto-blaster, through which* GURVINDER'*s original oath in Punjabi is being relayed. Silence, as oath finishes*.)

TOM: Jesus.

GURVINDER: (*Off; relayed*) Ten years. All friends, all friends. An oath. A pact.
(*He appears in the opening of the makeshift tent in a version of his classroom Sikh gear, the kirpan sheathed, a trail-mike in hand.*)

WAYNE: (*Tranced; back there*) Wow. Fuckin' Bruce Lee.

GURVINDER: (*Relay*) God's Armchair.

DAISY: Gotscam Chairs? What about it . . . ?
(*He draws the sword, points upwards. Their eyes follow, climbing rock to sky.*)

TOM: God's Armchair. Got it. Ha.

MONA: Hey, hang on, I'm not climbin' that bugger in the dark, not in this skirt I'm not . . .

GURVINDER: When it's time. We walk up. There's a path.

DAISY: And when's that, pray, O King?

GURVINDER: 4.42, accordin ' to t'Evenin' Post. (*Sword again.*) That's east. It's all laid on.

MONA: Wow.
(*They absorb it. Check reactions.*)

HESTER: Why?
(*Screech-owls; silence.*)

DAISY: Sandra's birthday.

WAYNE: Is it?

TOM: Ratface.

MONA: Yeah.

GURVINDER: (*Small smile, eyes fixed on her*) Because I love you.

HESTER: What?

GURVINDER: Because you are my friend.
(*A country clock begins to strike in the distance.*)
We have a mountain, a lake, a fire, food, drink . . .

DAISY: Ganga . . .

GURVINDER: . . . And each other.

MONA: (*Soft*) It's never ten years, is it?

GURVINDER: Life is good.
(*Black.*
Bring up: a fat gold moon. Then, in three pools of half-light:

99

TOM, *sitting;* DAISY, *prone, torching water beneath, on a ledge of rock a foot or two above the tarn;* HESTER *and* GURVINDER *by the fire, his head in her lap;* WAYNE *upright, his back to the base of the limestone stand;* MONA *crosslegged on a rock above him.*)

WAYNE: You know what's ironic? I spent six years breaking the law of the land on a regular basis as a policeman an' I get four years for an accident, there was no intention there, I was drunk and in a foul mood and she was holdin' 'im so tight I thought she'd crush him or something. So I . . . (*Shakes his head: a cul-de-sac*) When I say a life of total crime I'm merely being factual, you understand, I don't claim anything outa the ordinary, monthly sweeteners, the blind eye, the odd word, a bit of recycling, you know, dope 'n' stuff, beating up on awkward buggers in the cells, bending witnesses, lying in court . . . Nothing outside the generality of things, I was never a rotten apple . . . You know it really, but you don't want to know, right? Mm. Anyway. The bubble burst. The lights went out. I thought it'd last forever. Pop (*Beat.*) Click. (*Lights cut to half;* TOM's *and* DAISY's *up to full. Silence.* DAISY *stares hard into the torched water, her face wobbled by light.* TOM *carefully builds and rebuilds a delicate mound of small stones and pebbles.*)

DAISY: Here's the thing. I've just spent three months living rough with the homeless, OK? Manchester, Liverpool, Glasgow, Birmingham. We've put a mind-crushing film together. I mean . . . wow . . . special. Says it all. Only problem is: they won't put the bugger out. Too political. Lacks balance. They've put someone in to re-edit. Put the other point of view. Whatever that is . . . The poor are always with us? The homeless have only themselves to blame? It's pathetic. We sleepwalk into silence. The four Ms rule, OK. Murdoch, Maxwell, Marmaduke and Margaret. Got it all sewn up. Oh God, I met some beautiful people, too. Beautiful. (*Sudden.*) Fish.

TOM: (*Peering*) Where?

DAISY: (*Frowning*) Gone.

(*Lights to half;* HESTER's *and* GURVINDER's *to full.*)

HESTER: (*Stroking his head*) For myself I give you no argument,
  they've been good years, you know. I buckled down when I
  left school, played by the rules, winners and losers, good
  pickings, clean nose, capital city, my own company at
  twenty-five. Miss Enterprise Culture. I won't say I've ever
  really been taken in by it all, I'm black and a woman and
  that'll always give them problems, you know . . . But there
  were times I could even imagine myself being One of Us, my
  personal preferences a question of choice, not different from
  a car or a meal or a flat . . . Then, out of the blue, last year,
  they come up with this Clause 28 and . . . they meant it.
  They meant me. They meant me. So then I see I'm not One
  of Us at all. Just 'one of them'. (*Laughs.*) Clears the head. Oh
  yes.

GURVINDER: So. Is that a yes or a no?

HESTER: Come on, Gurvinder, I can smell your teases a mile
  off . . .

GURVINDER: I want to marry you. Yes or no?

HESTER: Gurvinder, I just told you, Clause 28, the Bill against
  Gays and Lesbians: I don't get off on guys, OK? Feel
  honoured I tell you. OK?

GURVINDER: You're telling me you're a dyke?

HESTER: I'm telling you I'm a dyke.

GURVINDER: Oh. I can see that'd be a problem. (*She strokes his
  head; loves him.*) I suppose a quick knee-trembler's
  completely out of the question . . . ?

  (MONA *laughs. Their lights to half,* MONA's *and* WAYNE's *to
  full.*)

MONA: 'S funny what they do to ye, parents. I was always the
  pretty one, me. Our kid was the brainy one. Upstairs an'
  downstairs, right? (*Thinks.*) But I tell ye, there's gotta be
  better than's happenin' to me. An' not just me, either, by
  God. It's not right. It's not. How I look's my business, I
  shouldn't 'ave to make a business of it. (*Thinks.*) I'm glad
  Sandra gorraway, I am. I'da gone with 'er, I would, I mighta
  fancied a bit o' travellin', meetin' folk. But I've got the kid to

think of now. Gorra gerrit right for her, no danger. So. (*Thinks.*) Ye do what ye can. Ye do what you 'ave to. Ye do what they let ye.

WAYNE: Funny how like the world a prison is. Hull was a bloody nightmare, o' course, they put me in with the puffs an' the other warped buggers 'cos o' my 'crime' so-called. (*Shudders.*) Sick every night for a month, I was. Thorp Arch though – the open prison – that was a dream, I tell you. All the drugs 'n' booze ye could handle an' sex to order (*Taps his nose*) when you learnt the ropes. Better class o' people, too, white collar, see, managers, executives, entrepreneurs, solicitors, financial advisors, the cream you might say, O and A levels, degrees, the lot, good crowd, you know, unlucky to be caught, the stuff that's goin' down out here ... Doin' business is what it's called out here, in court they call it fraud, see. Felt sorry for 'em, I did. Oh yes. (*Long pause.*) I don't blame Sandra leavin' me. (*His face reddens. Eyes moisten.*) I just don't understand why she left it till I was comin' out to tell me ...

(*Slow fade to half-light. Bring up* TOM's *and* DAISY's *light to full.* TOM's *upright, staring out across the tarn.* DAISY's *on her back watching him.*)

TOM: I went back, signed on for another tour, wrote my folks. Really felt I'd had it with this place. And. My pa got sick, retired from the service, '86? '86 ... I flew home, he popped it a couple of days later. But we did get to talk a little. I told him I loved him. He reminded me of my responsibilities and I didn't go back. Palestine wasn't real, wasn't possible. Hi-tech was both.

DAISY: (*Gentle*) Cheer up, kid. At least you didn't join the bloody Army ...

TOM: Right.

DAISY: So what is it you do?

TOM: (*Long pause*) Aviation. I work with planes.

DAISY: (*Looking him up and down*) I should've guessed that.

(*Lights to half; bring up* HESTER's *and* GURVINDER's *light to*

full. GURVINDER's *on his feet, staring east, eyes angry;*
somewhere else.)

HESTER: You pissed off with me?

GURVINDER: (*Returning; not turning*) What? No. Not with you.

HESTER: What then?

(*He shrugs, turns, pokes the fire with a stick.*)

DAISY: (*From half-dark*) Poor Gurvinder.

GURVINDER: Why'd'ye never call me Girlie?

HESTER: I can't bear to see men cry. I don't know. You gonna
tell me what's up?

GURVINDER: We could get married. We wouldn't have to live
together. I mean . . . we could just be there for each other.

HESTER: Like Sandra and Wayne? Come on, big eyes, you can
do better than that. (*Thinks it through a bit.*) Jesus, I don't
know the first thing about you, Gurvinder. You're weird
and beautiful and utterly opaque. Like, how come you're so
rich, you know? What are you? What do you do?

GURVINDER: What am I? I'm a businessman. What do I do? I
fuck the world.

MONA: (*Half-light*) Such a bloody waste. Everywhere ye look.

GURVINDER: Ye don't want to know.

HESTER: Try me.

GURVINDER: Open the bag.

(*He hands her a key. She opens the Gladstone. Stares at the*
contents.)

You're looking at a hundred thousand quidsworth
minimum, on the street. (*She looks up, stares at him.*)
There's fifty thousand quidsworth of E in the boot o' the
Bentley, another hundred thou of dope in the limo. So
what's it doing here? Well, according to extremely well-
sweetened sources in the Drug Squad, the new club is due a
raid in about . . . (*Watch*) ten minutes' time. (*Smiles.*) I
didn't get where I am today by not knowin' when I'm about
to be busted. These've bin the good years for us folk. The
folk who fuck the world. The Bag-Lady's done us proud.
Where there is discord, let there be profit. Where there is
error, let there be profit. Where there is doubt, may we

bring profit. Where there is despair . . . let there be smack.
Oh yes.

HESTER: (*Wide-eyed; in shock*) Gurvinder . . .

GURVINDER: They put me away. They lied. They shamed my
family. I cannot love these people. I cannot respect these
people.

HESTER: Oh God, Gurvinder, you can't even respect yourself . . .

GURVINDER: (*Tough, dark*) Who can? Who can? (*Silence.*) In
Borstal, I met some brothers . . . (*In their voice*) 'bahn in
Barbados' . . . they gave me a map of the world and a path
through it, ours and theirs, us and them. The world of the
Bag-Lady. And the Bag-Lady said, Let there be Wealth and
there was Wealth, and a half of the people fattened on it till
their bellies hung over their belts and their snouts glistened.
And the Bag-Lady said Let there be Poverty and there was
Poverty in spades, and anger and need stalked the land like
Little and Large on Angel Dust and the folk who fuck the
world cleaned up at both ends, shit and vomit, it's all one.
Listen. Business is deep. Business goes all the way down.
What do I do? I buy and sell. On top, above board, shares,
houses, land, water, gas, oil, phones, airplanes, firms,
futures. Below, underground, it's crack and smack and E
and tea and speed and feed and the tools that mark out the
turf (*Holds up his finger-shooter, bangs one off*). I'm doin' OK,
me. Except my family won't have me in the house, won't
even speak on the phone. Me dad. Me dad was the first Asian
building worker in Leeds. He's still got his first wage-packet.
'S true.

(*He pulls away from her searching eyes, pads off to stare at the
black nowhere to the east.*)

TOM: (*Toneless; remote*) I thought I'd write poems.

(HESTER *closes, locks the bag, lays the key on it. Moves towards
the awning, gathers the discarded trail-mike, as if to tidy it away,
doesn't.*

People have sifted back in, the light slowly altering to camp-site.
DAISY *comes to stand with* GURVINDER. *Rests her head on his
shoulder.*

HESTER *hums softly into the mike, finding the piece.* MONA
draws TOM *into a slow stiff-legged dance that barely moves.*
WAYNE *picks up the kirpan, flashes at the dark with it.*)
HESTER: (*Sings; slow torch version*) Hush
    Hush
    Somebody's calling my name . . .
    O my lord
    O my lord
    What shall I do . . .
    (*Fade to black.*
    Bring up: moon, still fat, smaller.
    Bring up: laughter, chat.
    Bring up: camp-fire, down to embers. They sit or sprawl around
    it, sharing joints and cans of lager.)
GURVINDER: (*Mid-tale*) . . . So he's never bin to London,
    Charlie, right? Hardly bin out of Heckmondwike. Two tons
    o' logs on the back. Time 'e gets there it's mornin',
    Edgware Road, not a soul up, he's no idea where 'e is . . .
    Sees an old feller walkin' the dog, he pulls up, he says is
    this London, flower? The guy says, Aye, you've made it.
    Charlie says, Oh that's gradely, where d'ye want the
    wood . . . ?
    (WAYNE *arrives with a major flask of coffee and cups.*)
WAYNE: Coffee, chief.
    (*People reach in for it.*)
GURVINDER: I've told ye, Wayne, don't keep callin' me Chief,
    people'll think I'm a fuckin' Indian . . .
WAYNE: Sorry, Boss.
GURVINDER: I've told ye about that daft hat as well . . .
WAYNE: 'S my uniform . . .
DAISY: Oh I wondered. Thought it might be costume . . .
MONA: (*Tasting coffee*) Oh God, no sugar . . .
WAYNE: Couldn't find sugar.
DAISY: (*Pointing*) There's sweeteners in my bag there . . .
    (WAYNE *lumbers off to find them.*)
MONA: Oh God, I'm knackered . . .
GURVINDER: (*Checking Rolex*) Not long.

DAISY: (*Imitating him*) Not long. Not long. God, you're such a
    fuckin' poser, Girlie . . .

GURVINDER: (*Grin*) I know.

DAISY: So what is it with you and this place, eh? Are you gonna tell
    us?

GURVINDER: I might.

    (WAYNE's *back with the Sweetex pills spread on a saucer, his idea
    of the style of things.*)

MONA: Oh don't. He'll just mek up more bullshit, ye know
    him . . .

WAYNE: I know what it is, he's told me already . . . (*Raises his
    hand, fingers extended. Glances at* GURVINDER.) Pantisabu,
    right?

GURVINDER: Panjisahib.

WAYNE: Right.

TOM: What about him?

WAYNE: 'S not an '*im*, 's'n *it*. 'S a handprint. In a rock.

MONA: More bullshit.

TOM: Whose?

WAYNE: (*A look at* GURVINDER) Some bigwig, begins with a G . . .

GURVINDER: Gurunanak.

MONA: Told ye.

WAYNE: Anyway, this guru bloke goes up on a big hill, limestone
    rock, to pray, see . . .

GURVINDER: Meditate.

WAYNE: Right. But there's a ganga nutters livin' up there an' they
    don't like him movin' in on their turf, like, so they decide to
    get shut of 'im, and their chief hurls this bloody great boulder
    straight at his head, right? But the guru bloke's meditating so
    'ard he's built up this kind of psychic wall around 'imself, see,
    so just by puttin' his 'and up like that, he stops the rock in
    mid-air, without even touchin' the bugger. (*Silence.*) And that
    rock's up there to this day. With the print of the guru bloke's
    hand on it.

    (*Silence. They look at each other.*)

TOM: Where?

WAYNE: On the rock.

TOM: (*Indicating*) Up there?

WAYNE: No, India, I think.

DAISY: Wait a minute, what the hell has this got to do with Gotscam and Girlie?

WAYNE: Search me.

DAISY: But that was the question, Wayne.

WAYNE: Was it? Oh.

GURVINDER: (*Soft*) Me dad brought us here, when I were a kid. Told me the story. Gurunanak. Panjisahib. (*Looks up at it.*) His dad'd teken 'im to see the real thing, back home. This place reminded him of it.
(*Silence.*)

MONA: This coffee's crap. Pass us another o' them sweeteners, will ye?
(DAISY *holds out the saucer. Begins to examine the pills intently.* TOM *checks the time on his watch.* DAISY *goes to fetch her bag.*)

GURVINDER: Time is it?

TOM: Half three.

GURVINDER: Nearly there.
(HESTER *pours more coffee. Sweeteners.*)

DAISY: (*Back*) Wayne, the sweeteners . . .

WAYNE: Oh aye, sorry, they're 'ere . . .
(*He hands them to her. Sees the bottle of Sweetex in her hand.*)
Oh, you've got two, have you . . . ?

DAISY: Oh shit. Who took sweeteners? (*Everyone.*) Oh shit.

HESTER: What?

DAISY: (*Handing bottle back*) What does that say, Wayne?

WAYNE: (*Squinting hard*) Mog. Mogga. Don. Mogadon. New one on me is that, aye.
(*Silence. Looks.*)

DAISY: Sorry, Girl.

GURVINDER: Duke.

WAYNE: Yes, chief?
(MONA *chuckles, draws sleeping bag up, rolls onto her side.*)

MONA: Right, that's me then.

GURVINDER: (*To* WAYNE) It's OK.

(*Slow fade.* GURVINDER *goes last. He sits on cross-legged, eyes fixed, resistant. Black.*
Bring up: alarm clock. It tails away.
Bring up: sound of a dozen or so bikes thundering along the bottom road towards the site.
Bring up: the camp-site. Bright day, around 9 o'clock.
The six lie like discarded dolls around the dead fire. The bikes stop by the cars; rev ominously; cut. A solitary rider continues, noses forward, appears on the edge of the site, leathers inscribed: Chapter One, *stops, takes in the scene, noses on, makes a slow searching circle of the sleepers, stops at the final figure of* WAYNE. *Removes helmet: it's* SANDRA, *long free bleached hair, utterly changed. She leans down to get a closer look.*
WAYNE *half-wakens for a moment. Stares up at her face.*)

WAYNE: Hello, San.

SANDRA: Hello, Wayne.

(*He's gone at once.* SANDRA *takes a final look at the group, returns her helmet, revs, rumbles off.*
The support bikes start up, throttle up, roar away.
Bring up: music: 'Every Time We Say Goodbye'.
Slow fade to black. Screen image of Thatcher, raddled, last days, on the crossfade. The song continues, calm, felt, as Poll Tax riots slowly burn out the Thatcher face.)

SONG: . . . When you're near there's such an air
    Of Spring about it . . .
    (*Begin slow mix through to image of Major.*)
      . . . I can hear a lark somewhere
      Begin to sing about it
      There's no vu more déjà
      Than the change so strange
      From Thatcher to Major . . .
    (*The note holds. Dies. Major holds.*
    Bring up: SANDRA, *bike, leathers, bleached hair flowing below helmet, on the road.*)

SANDRA: (*Sound effects down*) . . . I don't care if it *is* shit, it's my shit, not theirs. It's not semis and mortgages and pitbulls and *Blind Date* and poisoned water and salmonella and slaughter a few thousand foreigners when it all gets too much . . . Fuck *their* shit. (*Sounds up a moment, down again.*) You should try it, friend. The Road really earths you. Puts you in charge. Drivin' your own life. Give it a go, 'is all I'm sayin', what else are you doin' . . . What?

(*Crossing to:* TOM, *cockpit of Tornado, diving in for the turkey shoot (Highway 8), Gulf War, mute save for the clack and sput of control-intercom.*

At the end, mission complete, as he banks and peels, he's at last released into feeling, punches the air like a good 'un, tears streaming down cheeks and chin.

Fade.

The image of Major persists.

Bring up:)

VOICE: Britain should approach the millennium with head and spirits high. The prize is great, the hope invigorating, the dream attainable. We want, with you, to make the dream a reality.

(*Major fades.*

Bring up:)

TOM: (*Off*) The road to Basra. Highway 8. Next day. Sent back next day. Next day.

(*Bring up:* TOM's *face, frozen on screen, mouth open. A chittering burst on fast-forward, slows to play for a moment, we hear a phrase or two: 'Sent back. Fly over it . . .'. Freeze frame again, on midshot; he wears striped dressing gown over pyjamas, institutional setting.*

Bring up:)

PSYCHIATRIST: (*Off; dictating notes on the interview onto microtape*) Flight Lieutenant Thomas Peacock Clare . . . Post-combat stress trauma Grade VI . . . Trapanazene 6 grams per diem until further notice. Release date query. Await stabilization before release to community care . . .

(TOM *in, as the notes set up, directly below screen. He wears a long brown overcoat, ancient trousers, sandals, no socks. Carries a bag stuffed with his movables.*

TOM: The road to Basra. Highway 8. Next day. Sent back. Fly

over it. Camera. In a gunship. 200 feet. 200 feet. Smelling
them. Through the skin of the ship. Smelling them. Watch
out for vultures on the intercom. Thousands. In hover
pattern. Waiting their turn. Our people in the sand,
removing material, equipment. And for twenty miles the
road to Basra black and white with birds and bones,
untouched by our people in the sand. (*Touches head.*)
Untouched.

(*The screen image fades. He begins to shuffle off. Stops. Cocks
his head, assailed by his voices.*)

What? No. Ireland. Yes. What? I can't. No I can't, I don't
want to, I'm going to Ireland, my mum's people, country of
my mother and mother of all countries . . . Yes. Daisy?
Don't know. Not seen. No, no one. Poems? No. Don't do
poems, not real, not poss, old boy. (*Shouts.*) Ireland.
(*Blinks.*) The road to.

(*He goes.*

Bring up: WAYNE, *at bar, talking to disinterested barman. He's
in makeshift combat outfit.*)

WAYNE: No, so I got out of Security, loada crap, no discipline,
this place is really down the tubes, right? And I landed right
on my feet, all these fuckin' wars, excuse the language,
course the small-arms trainin' in the Force helped, like . . .
800 quid a week anywhere in the world and don't have to
travel to Africa to do it, 's right here on the doorstep. Great
job. Oh aye. Russia last month, Greece before that . . . Hey,
guess who I saw in Greece? D'you watch Sky News at all
. . . ? Daisy Jay, you know, the correspondent . . . She was at
the airport doin' an interview with some army chief,' course I
know 'er well, at school together, see, but. I didn't bother
'er, I could see she was busy. (*Stares at his drink.*) Great Job.
Dropped lucky. Aye.

(*Looks up. The guy has moved away. Looks down at his drink
again. Takes a sip.*)

Dropped lucky. Aye.

(*Crossing to:* DAISY, *on screen, rehearsing swishing hair from
side to side as she waits for action.*)

DAISY: (*Running lines*) New New'n'True does it for me. All over
the world . . .
(*The cameraman rehearses a pull to midshot, reveals her, in
flak-gilet and silk shirt, her trademark clip-board in one hand.*)
VOICE: (*On-floor; off*) Ready to go, Miss Jay?
DAISY: (*To camera, can to ear*) Mark, Daisy. Just let me get it
straight, you open with me covering the war in Byelorussia,
mix through to the format stuff, on to this bit here (*Shakes
hair*), slowed down bla-bla, and out with cabin shot me flying
in to Macedonia, right? Fine. Ready when you are. Hair all
right? (*Listens.*) That *would* be the end of the world . . .
What? Remember allure? I think of little else, darling . . .
VOICE: (*From floor; off*) Stand by now and, New New'n'True
Hairways, scene two take three. Action.
(*Screen sound cuts. She does her piece, remembers allure.*
DAISY *has walked on below. Watches briefly. Turns away.*
Approaches bare wood coffin. She wears a simple black dress,
carries a single rose: a seasoned thirty-two-year old child. The
DAISY *on the screen mutely continues, remembering allure.*)
DAISY: The old trout died before I could get there. Eighty-three
years of age, she was changing a front tyre on the Hebron
Road when her heart went. She called me from the hospital
to tell me not to come. I'll go when I'm ready, she said, and
you've got work to do, my little peacenik.
(*Camera fades to black on screen. She stops to lay the rose on the*
coffin. Lights the two candles at either end. Stands.)
Daisy Jay, Sky News, Haifa, on the road, signing off.
She goes.
Bring up: HESTER *and* MONA *singing:* '*How Great Thou Art*', *a*
line each.
Bring up: screen. A faceless Tory leader, an election favour in his
lapel: Minor, perhaps.
HIS VOICE: (*Off*) In the last seventeen years. The Conservative
Dream. Millennium. In the last seventeen. Stuck to the
road. Conservative Dream. To the. Stuck. To the road. Your
dream. Safe in our hands. To the road . . .
(*Song ends. Minor fades.*

Bring up: HESTER, MONA, *coffin, candles. A hubbub of folk about the house, dominoes, shouts from the men, talk and reminiscence from the women, laughter from the kids: Nine Night, a Caribbean funeral custom.*
The two women kneel side by side before a sea-trunk, sorting Mrs Patterson's things. Clothes and objects on the floor about them. House sounds fade to low: still there.)

MONA: (*Gazing at framed photograph*) . . . God, this must be the wedding party in Kingston, just before they left. (HESTER *leans in to study it with her.*) Look at me dad. (*They chuckle.*) She was so beautiful.

HESTER: She was going to be a teacher.

MONA: Gerroff.

HESTER: She was.

(HESTER *returns to sorting.* MONA *looks on at the picture a moment.*)

MONA: I never thought of her as brainy.

(HESTER *opens up the scrunched-up Crimplene housecoat, hands it to* MONA.)

HESTER: Put that with throw-outs . . .

(MONA *takes the coat, studies it, feels it with her face, smells it. Stands as if to discard it; slips it on. Gradually finds her large, heavy, powerful, exhausted mother. Sits heavily on a stool by* HESTER, *addresses her.*)

MONA: (*Jamaican*) Come here, Mona girl, I'll do your hair while I've a minute . . .

(*She draws* HESTER *to her. Begins to do her hair. Talks to her throughout; of fatigue, of the family, of meeting her father, of the hospital, of hopes for* MONA; *of the pretty one.*)

Pickney gal – come here, let me comb your hair while me a sit down. Did you nah grease you scalp this morning, me nah want no dry head pickney you know. Got to feel the comb walk the scalp. Teck your hand out your hair. You is a Virgin Mary tonight eeh – you gwhen look sweet. And Hester is a what, wise person, a not a wise person – a wise man! I don't know if I can come tonight me can't teck another night off work, perhaps your daddy gwhen come,

but him going be tired. (*Finishes hair.*) Nee go set the table I
gwhen lie down little while.
(*She relaxes slowly back into herself. Smiles.* HESTER's *crying.*
They hug. Stay close.)

HESTER: You know something? I used to go to bed every night
when I was a kid and pray for a sister.

MONA: Did ye? I used to pray for a blonde wig.

HESTER: She loved you a lot.

MONA: She loved us both. Big heart. Right?

HESTER: Big heart. Right.

(*They return to the trunk. Work on. House noise up a little.*)
(*Factual; non-declaratory*)

Name: Elizabeth Rose Patterson
Date of Birth: 4/5/35
Country of Birth: Jamaica
Occupation: Hospital ancillary; various

MONA: Cause of death: coronary infarct.

Related factors: racial abuse, precipitating heart failure.

HESTER: Ambulance response time: 53 minutes.

MONA: Hospitals refusing admission: three.

HESTER: Hospital admission time: 2 hours 20 minutes.

MONA: Other comments:

HESTER/MONA: Dead before diagnosed.

(*Their lights slowly fade.*
GURVINDER *appears above them, buttoned Indian jacket,
trousers, by the screen, a box of virtual reality cartridges in his
hand. He kneels to feed them into his computers, checks each
image in turn as it's fed onto the screen:* WAYNE, SANDRA,
HESTER, MONA, DAISY, TOM, *all in their thirties. He stands,
touches a sensor, bringing up lights on the penthouse apartment
below to which he now descends. A TV in an adjacent, otherwise
empty room flickers greyly: a New Year's party for the
millennium.*
*The viewing room he's reached is also empty, save for the screen
and a great moulded chair facing out. He gathers a VR visor and
glove from the arm of the chair, puts them on; sits; fingers console.
The lights dip. Fingers it again. The screen comes to life again:*

the image of Gotscam. He moves the glove, the image becomes a
close-up section of the ledge, the Chair itself.
Midnight in the next room. Chimes. Cheers.
Lamps appear in the dark of the ledge, figures. DAISY's *Angel*
Gabriel, TOM's *Joseph,* MONA *and* SANDRA's *Marys,*
HESTER's *Wise Person,* WAYNE's *Innkeeper,* GURVINDER's
King. They begin speaking their lines from the nativity play,
detached and not quite human voices seeking no connection.
White light slowly grows on the ledge: sun rise; power restored.
They abandon the lines; piano and guitar set up, leading them
into 'Mr Sunnyman'.
The song ends. They stare on, as white light reaches GURVINDER
in his chair.
He glares hard through the visor, staring into the light.)

GURVINDER: (*Fierce; low; echoic; relayed*) I don't know if you
know. Or if you care. But this place is turning. Into shit. I
don't know if you know. Or if you care. But you fucked up.
We. You're going to have to start again. We. Start again.
(*He reaches into his jacket pocket, takes out the marble-bag,*
holds it out in the palm of his hand. Opens it. Draws out the
scissored Sikh braids. Holds them out.)
For a start. How do I get this back on?
(*Silence. The white light slowly fades, screen above and chair*
below.)
I don't hear you. I don't hear you.
(*The ungloved hand touches the console.*
Fast fade to black.)